Running a Successful Business after the Start-up Phase
or, Who are you Calling Mature?

Preface

Welcome to my guide to running a successful business after the start-up phase, something that I'm doing right this minute.

Why did I write it? I published my first business book, *How I Survived my First Year of Full-Time Self-Employment: Going it Along at 40*[1] in 2013. I got a really good response to it (see the Appendices for more information and some reviews), including lots of comments about how different it was from other start-up books.

A year down the line, I was doing well and feeling like I had a mature business on my hands. What do I consider to be a mature business? Read on to find out. But when I went to look for books on this topic, there were very few. It's all about the start-up – and for some traditional entrepreneurs, who want to jump from start-up to start-up, relishing the excitement and scares of very new businesses, that's fine. But what about people who want a stable, not-quite-so-exciting time but aren't quite sure how to get there?

I'd been blogging my progress through the more mature side of business and I decided to pull some of those posts together into themes to share with you how I balance my life, get clients, keep clients, and (even!) get rid of clients . I'm going to talk about investing in your business: how to know when to invest, how to assess your return on investment, and how to know when not to invest. Blogging has been a major driver of clients to my services and readers to my books, so I decided to include a section on blogging, covering all of those basics that people assume you know … and then I realised that people probably do still need an introduction to social media, too, so popped some brand new information in there.

---

[1] http://librofulltime.wordpress.com/e-book-going-it-alone-at-40/

If you've read my previous book, you'll know that everything I write about is drawn from my own personal experience. I do pull in information, advice and experiences from other people from time to time, but it's all based on my business. However, even though I'm an editor, proofreader and transcriber, I've worked hard to make this book relevant to anybody who freelances or runs a small business, whatever they do. So don't be put off by the fact that I'm an editor – anyone from a roofer to a drain engineer, from a typist to a voiceover artist, will be able to find something useful here.

Yes, it's a business guide, but it's about my personal experience of running a business which is well into profit, enabling me to have a comfortable and balanced lifestyle — an income and a life. Who doesn't want that? It's a bit less personal than my first book (and there are fewer cardigans) but I'll guide you through the steps that I took and be your friend and companion on the next part of your business journey …

Come with me and find out what a mature business is, if you've got one, and, if not, how to get one. Enjoy!

Contents

How to use this book

You can read this book all the way through in one go, or move to sections that particularly interest you. It's up to you and the point that you've reached in your business journey. Each section has an introductory section under the main heading, and I recommend scanning through those to get an idea of what I'm talking about.

Links

The practical, instructional chapters in this book include links to blog posts on my website at www.libroediting.com where you can access bonus material such as screenshots of the processes I'm talking about in that chapter. This book doesn't include many screenshots, as screenshots are notoriously difficult to provide in a useful way in printed books of this size. I've got around this issue by giving you text instructions here in this book, and also links to the relevant online articles, where you can see lots of screenshots.

I will give you the full link in a footnote at the bottom of the page. Type that link into your browser when you're using your PC, laptop or mobile device and you will be able to view the blog posts, screenshots or other bonus material that I mention.

This is not mandatory – any blog posts that I link to include extra material that complements the material in this book, and the practical instructions that I include here have been tested and should be comprehensive enough to allow you to follow them and achieve the required results, but it will enhance your reading and learning experience.

Enjoy reading this book …

Acknowledgements

Thanks so much to Chrys Schlapak and Catherine Fitzsimons for being my beta readers and editors. It's scary putting out a book when you're an editor yourself, and I really appreciate your input. Thanks to Mr. Libro, Matthew (and I'm looking forward to becoming Mrs. Matthew in 2014!) for cheerfully taking second place to the business on occasion, but cheering me on all the way. Thanks to my peer group – Katharine, Laura, Louise, Linda and everyone else who I meet at the virtual watercooler. And thanks to the readers of my other books and to everyone who reviews this one!

Introduction: How do you know when you're running a mature business?

Lots of posts and books and blogs and courses and STUFF have been written about starting a new business. But what about when that phase is over? Some people, especially, it seems, in the technology sector, like to bounce from start-up to start-up, selling the business on or changing it in some way as soon as it has settled down. But what if you're in the one business for the long run? How do you tell when you've moved from the start-up phase to running a mature business?

What is it like running a start-up business?

In my experience, the first few years of running your own business are characterised by:

Uncertainty – will I get customers, will I keep customers, where will my next customers come from?

Active marketing – trying different marketing methods, signing up for directory websites, trying some adverts

Overwork – working all the hours there are for clients who need everything now! It's also possible that you're working at a day job while developing the business on the side

Underpay – thinking "can I actually charge for this? That much? Really?"

Constant change – changing strategy, changing business model, changing clients, changing business cards

A change in lifestyle and your social life – especially if this is your first start-up, you'll disappear from your friendship groups, become invisible to your family, and probably start hanging out with new business chums as well

What is it like running a mature business?

I'm in Libro's fifth year now, and things are markedly different from when I started. I know a few people who are just starting out, which helps me remember what it was like and see the differences. Here's what it's like once you're up and running

Certainty – much less worry about where customers are coming from; working with regulars who you know well, knowing their payment schedules and how they operate

Less marketing – many more jobs come from repeat clients and recommendations, so marketing is more about brand awareness and making sure that people know you're there, rather than grasping for new clients all the time

Steady work – you have reclaimed your evenings and weekends

Steady pay – you have worked up your rates of pay to industry standards, and are confident that what you do is worth what you charge for it (however, you might be on tax payment on account[2] if you're in the UK, which can be a slightly tricky transition)

Less change – while you still check for return on investment, buy the new technology you need to run your business and keep up with your personal development, things should be more stable, changing when you choose to change them

You get your life back – you can go back to your friends and family, but you also have a peer group of people in your industry who you can use as a mutual support group

---

[2] http://libroediting.com/2012/04/05/tax-payment-on-account/

How do you get from start-up to mature business?

These are some things that I've done, which I think are the key processes in this move:

Outsource some functions of the business – design and accountancy are key ones that I've done, but you might go ahead and outsource all of your admin functions

Optimise your customer base — so you have good, reliable, regular customers who bring in a good rate of return

Organise your work so that most of it comes from regulars who book it in advance, and have a system to record what you've got booked in so you can fit new work around it (I use a simple Gantt chart[3])

Turn away work and recommend it on rather than taking on anything and everything

Build a good network of peers who you can pass work to and from whom you can get advice and support or just a laugh or a rant occasionally (especially important if you work on your own)

Find the time and resources to **give something back** – when I was talking about growing a mature business on social media, someone pointed out that another feature is that you find yourself advising people on how to do it! Indeed, this is one of the main benefits of running a mature business for me, and this is what I've done …

- I wrote a post on how to become a proofreader[4] which ended up as a whole careers section[5] on my website, because so many people were asking me how to do it

---

[3] http://libroediting.com/2010/08/26/keeping-organised/
[4] http://libroediting.com/2011/10/26/proofreading-as-a-career/
[5] http://libroediting.com/blog/careers-advice/

- I wrote a book[6] on my first year as a full-time self-employed business person
- I share the knowledge I've gained of social media by volunteering[7] at Social Media Surgeries helping community groups to learn how to use Twitter, etc.
- I am informally mentoring a few colleagues through their first years as self-employed editors

---

[6] http://librofulltime.wordpress.com/e-book-going-it-alone-at-40/
[7] http://librofulltime.wordpress.com/2013/10/15/helping-at-the-social-media-surgery/

Developing your customer base

When you first start your business, you'll take any clients you can get. Sad, but true; and necessary, too. As you go along, though, you need to get more picky about who you take on as a customer, for both their sake and yours. It's no use taking on five customers who need to be able to send you work and have it done NOW: odds are that they'll all ask at the same time and you'll drive yourself into the ground while inevitably letting someone down.

In this section, I'm going to share with you my tips for getting freelance work in the first place, choosing the right clients to work with from the outset in order to avoid potential costly and upsetting mistakes, then look at refining your portfolio of clients so that you:

- Make more money
- End up with a good mix of clients
- Know who to work with and who NOT to work with again
- Turn one-off customers into regular customers

How do I get freelance work in the first place?

These are some ways that I've found successful in getting freelance work. They're applicable to all forms of freelance work but what we're not talking about here is getting a full-time employed job in whatever field.

It's also worth noting here that this is a suite of options and you wouldn't expect to do them all at the same time. Once you've started to use 1 and 2, you can pick and choose depending on what your career path is – and it's important to devote time to some planning from the start.

1. Make sure that you say what you do on your website

Many of your clients will come to you after performing a search online. Remember: people will take the easy option. Why bother to trawl through lists and directories if you can just Google?

So it's worth making sure that your website:

Includes a clear list of all of the services you offer

Includes a blog which is updated regularly – this really helps your position on the search results

Is Search Engine Optimised throughout (there is an art to this, but make sure you include your keywords regularly, write lots of natural reading text and include keywords in page / post titles and headings)

Includes a picture of you and ways to contact you – a contact form is always good for this

Oh yes – do make sure that you HAVE a website. Even if it's just one page, I really do think that in all industries, from carpentry to computer programming, people expect you to have some kind of web presence, and may well give up the search there and then if you don't, even if you've been recommended by name by someone. I know that I do that when I'm looking for services …

2. Make sure that people know what you do

An awful lot of my early clients came through friends of friends and social networks. Obviously, don't bombard your friends by begging them to refer you, but make sure that the following are covered:

- If you have a company Facebook page, include a list of your services
- If you use Twitter, include your services and links on your profile
- Mention what you do on social networks every now and again (a good way to do this is to mention what you've *been* doing: "This month I've edited this, transcribed that and localised the other"
- Make sure peers in one area know you cover other areas, too (if you do), e.g. I make sure that my editing chums know that I transcribe as well
- Consider setting up a newsletter and making sure you mention all of your services
- Update your clients with any new services you're offering

3. Join industry groups and publicise yourself through their directories

I gained early clients through being in a member directory associated with a copyeditors' email list. Friends do well by being listed on the Society for Editors and Proofreaders' website. My roofers are listed on a government-accredited tradespeople's website. All of these are places where people will look for accredited and approved suppliers.

4. Advertise on general directories and websites

A hint: don't bother with paid ones when there are so many free directories and websites!

Ask around your peers as to what they find useful. I am on Freeindex and get a few enquiries a month. Join as many as you want, but do make sure to update your profile if you change your services, fees, etc.

If you're in a trade like roofing or plumbing, it's worth looking at council and government-approved listings and the paid directories, as people do search these first, but beware putting too much money in to begin with.

Again, for trades, local print directories and especially business association directories can be good. I have a free listing in our local business association one, which has never brought me any work, but I always try to find local tradespeople who are members, and other people will do this, too.

5. Use industry-specific freelancer sites

I've had a look at general websites like freelancer.com, elance.com and oDesk.com and personally, I don't think they're worth it. A lot of people on those will undercut and take any job at the lowest price possible. Many of the sites have 'tests' which are actually a test of your understanding of the site itself, not your ability as a writer, graphic designer or whatever. Some friends tell me that elance.com is the best out of these. However, they have recently merged with oDesk, so time will tell there. Just beware, and don't end up working for almost nothing when there are other sources of jobs out there.

However, there are industry-specific freelancer sites which are worth it. Again, ask your peers for recommendations. The one that's got me the most work is proz.com, which is a site for translators where you can put up a profile and, if you pay for membership, that profile will be sent to people looking for freelancers, and they will contact you direct. This has paid back the membership fee for me tens of times over, because I work with translators into English, and offer localisation, which is related to translation.

You can also look for people looking for particular skills and freelancers and then pitch to them.

Take note, though: with anything you pay for, do assess each year whether you've got that fee back, and more. Only continue paying if you're getting a good return on your investment (see the next section for more on this)!

6. Advertise (selectively)

I'm not a big fan of paying out for adverts. Most of the other methods I talk about here are free. But there might be specific advertising channels that will work for you.

When I was starting out, working as a proofreader on theses and dissertations, I put up some posters around the university where I worked, recruiting colleagues who were also students to put them up in common rooms, etc. (free, except for printing costs and a few coffees!) and I advertised in the university staff newsletter, which went to tutors and supervisors. The costs were low, even to non-staff, and I did get the money back.

As with using websites that you pay for, do check your return on investment and keep an eye on the outgoings.

7. Use social media proactively

This one particularly applies to Twitter, although LinkedIn can be used in this way, too. Search for people looking for your services on Twitter. Reach out to potential clients directly. I have got paid work using this method and, even better (see below), I've got clients who have gone on to be big recommenders this way, too.

No one minds one, polite Tweet if they've asked for recommendations for a good plasterer or translator and you fit the bill. Don't hassle people and don't blanket-tweet; do tailor your response to the person you're contacting.

Have a look at Appendix 1 for a detailed guide on how to search for a job on Twitter.

8. Seek recommendations and referrals from clients

The best way to get new clients is through word of mouth. The two main advantages:

It's free!

If person A recommends you to person B, and person B gets in touch with you, they are far more likely to convert into a paying customer than someone who's randomly got in touch with you through an ad or Google search.

You do need to be a bit proactive about this, though:

- Make sure that your clients know you're looking for more clients just like them
- Say thank you whenever you find out someone's recommended you
- Ask clients for references to put on a reference page on your website (this makes enquirers more likely to use you as you come recommended by lots of people)

I have several clients who act as 'nodes' for me, recommending me either individually or via blog posts and pages on their websites.

9. Seek recommendations from your peers

Your peers fall into two groups:

1. People who freelance or run small businesses like you, who you might meet in online groups or at networking events
2. People in the same industry as you, who you might meet in the same ways

It's important not to see people in the same industry as you as competitors – you're much better off considering one another as colleagues. When I was starting out, I was passed what turned out to be a major client by a proofreader friend who wanted to stop working at weekends and in the evenings. So I did evening and weekend cover for them. Now I'm established, I much prefer to be able to recommend potential clients who I can't take on to another qualified person who I know will do a good job, rather than simply telling them that I can't do it.

When you're starting out, it's worth forging (genuine) relationships with people in your industry who are more established. They may well have the odd customer they want to pass on, or have too much business and be looking for people to recommend on to. Nowadays, I pass people I can't accommodate on to a core set of five or so recommended proofreaders, writers and transcribers. I also keep a note of people in allied industries such as book design, graphic design in general and indexing, so I can pass clients to them with a relevant recommendation, as an added bonus to save them from having to seek these people out.

You can also profit from either teaming up with peers in different industries. For example, I've worked with web designers on projects where they've written the website and I've provided the content, and I've done proofreading work for virtual assistants who don't offer that service themselves.

I haven't got many clients directly through networking, but I met an author at an event who went on to recommend my transcription services to a fellow author, who now uses me for transcription and editing, AND recommends me on her website!

10. Go cold calling and door-knocking

Some people do cold-calling and door-knocking, where they literally call people on the phone or walk up their front paths and ask them for work. For a start, I don't think that works in the service industry. I feel this takes a LOT of investment. Cold calling requires a list, which takes time and research or money to get, and taking time out to walk up a lot of paths is a fairly hefty investment, too. It might be more worthwhile looking at trade directories or local directories before you take this path.

However, when I wrote about this on my website, I did have quite a few responses from people who have had success with cold-calling or writing speculative letters to prospective clients, so it's worth giving it a go if you've got the time and resources.

How do I make more money?

So, you're running a freelance business – whether you're a plumber, a roofer, an IT specialist, an editor or whatever, and you want to make more money. Of course you do. How do you do it? Short of putting all of your prices up (which is something you can often actually do, especially if you've been undercharging for years), here's what I see as the best ways to make more money in your freelance business.

Put your prices up!

Well, I don't mean this quite as bluntly as that. But when we start a business, we often doubt ourselves, and don't have the confidence to charge industry standard rates. "Oh, I'm new, this customer deserves a cheaper rate". "I don't know what I'm doing, so I'd better charge low". "I might get the business if I quote lower than everyone else, I can always raise it later". Sound familiar? Well …

If you really don't know what you're doing, you shouldn't be charging people for your work. But if you're just unsure of yourself, and you've had feedback that your work is OK, don't put yourself down (I'm afraid that I have heard this more from women than men. Why, ladies, why?)

Check what the industry standard rates are (look at trade associations, other people's websites, if you have a mentor in the business, ask them what they charge) and base your charges on those

If you do give a discount, give it for another reason than because you're new – for example, I give discounts to students and individuals self-publishing their books

If you do give an introductory discount, make the customer pay in another way – the best is by giving you a reference to put on your website and marketing material

Get organised!

If you want to work more and make more money per hour, then you have to work smarter. This falls into two sections:

Organise your admin – streamline your admin processes, organise yourself so that your systems tell you what to do next and automate your invoicing, OR outsource your accounts, invoicing or all of your admin to someone expert in the task.

Organise your paid work – make sure that you're using the latest software, aids, short cuts, materials, whatever it takes to make your work in your industry as speedy and efficient as possible

Specialise!

In every line of work, there's general work (replacing roofs) and there's specialised work (matching slates, doing repair work, conservation). Find what specialities match your skills, and you'll find that the more specialised the work, the higher your rates can be.

You would expect to pay more for a carpenter who designs and makes you a bespoke kitchen than for one who puts together a flat pack you've bought from a DIY store (or you'd expect to pay the same carpenter more for the first task)

Lots of people do editing work – I specialise in non-native English speakers, and I can charge a premium for my experience in this area

Do be careful – make sure that you really are an expert before you go charging extra for expert services. Prospective clients will want to see evidence of your ability if they're going to pay you more, so write down your experience on your marketing materials and collect some testimonials.

Diversify!

Isn't this the opposite of specialising, I hear you ask. Well, to an extent. But consider this:

Having worked with overseas students' dissertations and theses, I diversified into working with translators who are translating from their native language into English. It's still non-native English, and I'm still making it sound like native English, but I'm working for professional organisations, so the student discount need no longer apply.

I used my audio-typing training to diversify into transcription. Some of the work I do in this area is more lucrative than others, but I wouldn't have this income stream at all if I hadn't diversified (and I get a good return on investment for it, too – see the section on Investing in your business for more on this)

I used my experience working for the UK office of an American company to branch out into localisation services – often done for large agencies and companies who reward this specialist area (see point above, too)

My handyman, Terry, extended his range of services when he made me some window screens and realised there are lots of people out there who need such things. Another string to his bow – and something he can do when it's raining and he can't paint the outsides of people's houses.

Making more money in your freelance business

You can see that by matching the industry's rates first of all, then streamlining your processes and simultaneously specialising and diversifying, you can up your rates of pay while working the same hours.

How do I decide who to work with?

When you're new to your freelance career, it's tempting to rush around picking up every job you can. But it's really worth evaluating the companies with whom you choose to work, from the very beginning. At the very least, you can avoid making yourself uncomfortable or making a small amount of money for a large amount of time. At the most extreme, you can avoid losing money, or even breaking the law! Read on for my hints and tips ...

Do conduct background checks

When a company contacts you to book you for a job, it's easy to say yes without thinking. But it's always good to do a few basic background checks:

- If the company has found you through a professional organisation or website that has discussion boards or feedback mechanisms, check what other people have said about the company
- Run a Google search for [company name] and phrases such as "bad payer", "didn't pay", "don't work with"
- Ask your peers or any networks you're in (on and offline) about whether they've worked with them before

I love it when a company approaches me via Proz, a jobs website I belong to, because members can see peer reviews of companies that are also members. The only time I've had a problem with a company that booked me through Proz was when I forgot to look at their peer-reviewed listings and assumed that they'd be OK.

Do check what they say on their website

This can tell you a lot about the company that wishes to book you. Is their website professional? Does it have terms and conditions? If it's an agency itself, does it seem to offer fair terms to its clients (and what's the difference between what it charges its clients and what it's offering to pay you – always interesting!).

You can also find massive red flags by doing this. A friend, new to the editing business, told me that they were doing tests for a company that offered student proofreading. When we had a look at their website, they were boasting that their rewriting service was able to bypass plagiarism-detecting software! Of course, it's not ethical to rewrite student work – so we could see immediately that this was NOT a good company to work for. (If you're considering going into student editing / student proofreading via agencies, it's worth reading the Choosing a Proofreader: Student Edition article[8] on my blog and using that to help you decide who to work with.)

This brings me nicely on to the next point …

Don't do something that goes against your ethics – or the law!

Is it worth undermining your own ethics to make a bit of cash? I don't think so, personally. One, you're going to feel uncomfortable about what you're doing, and two, it might come back and bite you later. I certainly wouldn't want to work with the company I talk about in the above point, and I also wouldn't want my name to be associated with any company I wouldn't be proud to be associated with!

I've turned down jobs for companies that operate in areas I'm not personally comfortable with (someone writing a website in order to attract people in the sex industry to his professional services springs to mind), and I have certainly turned down work for SEO and linking farms, which I don't agree with as a concept. I've never been asked by a company to write an essay for a client, but I know that I'd say no if I was asked. If you search online, you can find articles by

---

[8] http://libroediting.com/2013/09/18/choosing-a-proofreader-for-students/

people who work for content farms, or write fake reviews of products for money, or write essays for people and feel they can justify it, so it's not black and white, but do stick with your own boundaries and don't upset yourself by crossing them.

I have written text for marketing websites that I find to be a bit cheesy and I am not exactly hugely proud of it. But they don't tell any lies, and it was 'white label' work (i.e. my name is not on it). That doesn't mean that I'd go against my ethics if my name wasn't on something, though!

Do go to the edge of your comfort zone; don't cross out of it

I took on my first transcription job as a "why not?" kind of test – but I did have audio typing training, so I knew that the skills involved would be close to ones I already had (I wrote an article about what happened next[9]). I also once took on a job doing some audio recording for a website that needed an English accent. I didn't really have the experience or equipment to do this and, although I did a decent job, I turned down further requests to do this kind of work Because the return on investment and the professionalism of the job I was able to do didn't match my expectations .

So do push yourself a bit and move into new areas by all means, but don't jump too far in one go.

Don't do (too much) work for free

I will do a test for a company for free, but not more than one, small job. I do do the odd bit for other start-ups or local small businesses, to help them out, but nowadays I don't do anything for free for a commercial company.

---

[9] http://libroediting.com/2013/03/20/career-in-transcription/

Even if you do end up doing something 'for free' for a company while you're building your client base and establishing your reputation, make sure up front that they will supply you with a testimonial / reference with their name and company name that you can publish on your website if you do a good job for them. This does give you some sort of return for the work.

It's also OK to do work for a 'skills exchange' – I wrote some marketing materials for someone who designed some graphics to use on my site. Don't do too much of that, though, as the tax man can get quite interested in that sort of thing …

The main point is, you don't want to end up labouring away at unpaid work and – heaven forbid – turning away paid work because you've got to get the project finished!

Do ask for recommendations

Hopefully you'll have been building networks and contacts in your area of work. I have lots of colleagues to whom I can turn for advice, and I have a few colleagues who are just starting out in full-time editing businesses. I'm happy to ask them for holiday, sickness and I'm-too-busy-help cover, and I've also passed on some of my clients to them. As my client base has matured, I've had to move away from some of my clients who needed me to be able to drop everything to do work for them on a tight deadline, regularly. However, someone starting out, who might be a little less fully booked, was ideal to take them on.

It's always worth asking colleagues if they would like some holiday or sickness cover, or just establish mentoring kinds of relationships that will promote this kind of thing. Hopefully, the clients who your colleague passes to you will be decent payers and good clients (otherwise you might want to look at your choice of colleagues!), so you're less likely to get burnt.

Do check your return on investment

When you've done some work for a new client, and they've (albeit eventually) paid you, then do take the time to monitor the project and check for return on investment. For example, I always think that a client who sends you several small jobs a month and always pays on time is better than one who sends you a few big jobs but always needs chasing for payment. How much time are you wasting on chasing for payment? Here's how I tell if a client is worth working with again:

- Were they decent and easy to deal with?
- Did they communicate effectively with you?
- Did they pay on time? (The payment schedule might be a long one, but did they match it?)
- Was the work interesting? (this can matter, although at the start and through your career, you will need to accept that sometimes it just isn't!)
- Are you proud to be associated with this work / client?

If you can answer yes, then they're good at working with freelancers (I've written an article with more detail[10]) and hopefully you've got yourself a regular client – try to keep hold of them and make sure you say thank you for their payment and express interest in working with them again.

If they:

- Didn't resolve any project teething problems in good time
- Made you feel uncomfortable with what they asked you to do
- Didn't communicate with you and answer questions
- Didn't pay / paid late

---

[10] http://libroediting.com/2012/09/12/top-ten-tips-for-working-with-freelancers/

… those are red flags and, even if you're just starting out and you feel you're desperate for clients, I'd have a good think about whether to work with them again.

Do listen to your gut feeling

On most of the occasions when I've had trouble with clients and have made a bad decision about working with one, I've found that I had a gut feeling that it wasn't a good idea. If you get a gut feeling, by all means back it up with some of the ideas above, but do listen to it, and save yourself hassle and possibly heartbreak!

When it comes down to it, we all want clients who:

- Pay well and on time
- Have interesting and regular work to do
- Are likely to become regular clients

These tips and hints will hopefully help you to end up making good choices about the companies with which you work.

How do I turn a new customer into a regular customer?

Whatever field you're working in, having a stable of good, reliable, regular clients who send you work, are good communicators and pay decent rates in good time is a good place to be. The kind of client you want as a regular is the kind of client who follows all of the rules in the previous chapter. You may have chosen to work with them based on those criteria I've just talked about.

Here are some ways to help you turn a good first-time client into a trusted regular.

Do a good job the first time

This one's a bit obvious, but it's worth saying. Do a good job the first time, and you're likely to create a regular client just like that!

Be memorable for your good customer service

Leave the client with a good final impression. I'm always sure to say thank you for their payment and to wish them well with the publication / website / new service / novel / whatever it is that you've done for them this time.

Make sure that your client knows you'd like to work with them again

When I send my thank you for their payment, I make sure that I make it clear that I'd like to work with them again. Something along the lines of "I'm looking forward to working with you on future projects" will set a good note.

Remind the client that you're available

When you're establishing a relationship with a client, the odd little email reminder of your availability is fine (obviously don't hassle them). If you have a newsletter, asking them if they'd like to be added to your mailing list and sending them a monthly newsletter can keep you in their mind.

Make sure that clients know about all of your services

If, like me, you offer more than one service, make sure that your clients know this, too. I've got several long-term customers who use me for more than one service – one has moved from using my transcription services to using me as an editor (I also still transcribe for them) and a few use me for editing and localisation. Even if they only do one thing themselves, it's useful for people to know your range, so they can recommend you to their colleagues.

Offer an incentive

Once I have completed a job for a new customer and they've paid me successfully, I offer then an incentive. No, not money off! But I will usually offer to invoice them for all of the jobs I do for them in a month, at the end of the month. Win for them: they are given longer to pay and will receive one invoice for several jobs. Win for me: I only have to produce one invoice and record one payment, and I can add them to my monthly invoice run.

Note: make sure you are clear that this is an offer and they don't have to take it up. If they don't want to do this, make a note and invoice them as they like it to be done.

Thank them for their repeated custom and treat regulars well

I regularly tell my regulars how much I appreciate their regular custom and I treat them well in as many other ways as I can, too:

- I make it clear that at busy times, I will prioritise their work over new work (and I tell new prospects this, too – I think it gives a good impression to let everyone know that I treat my regulars well).

- I will also go above and beyond, doing a super-fast turnaround or working late to fit a job in – not to the detriment of other clients or my own health and sanity, but I treat them as well as I can.
- If I'm booking holiday or other time off, I will email my regulars in advance to warn them, so they don't just find out when they get my out of office reply.
- I will offer regulars a named holiday cover contact who they can work with when I'm not available, and introduce them to a trusted colleague if they wish me to.

This is how I have converted one-off customers into a group of regulars who bring me steady work and income, and peace of mind in knowing I've got a stable business. It's also how I make sure that I keep them!

What is the best mix of customers to have?

If you've got a mature business that is up and running and busy, then you've probably already used some of the criteria for getting new customers and the ways to turn those new customers into regulars that I've already talked about. But here's the golden question: what is the best mix of customers to end up with?

Obviously, in an ideal world, all of your jobs as a freelancer would be fun, interesting and high-paying, for clients who pay up on time. But we're not in an ideal world. The paying on time thing is non-negotiable for me (although I'm always prepared to listen if an otherwise reliable and exemplary client is having cash-flow problems, IF they tell me about them), but I've learned to live with the fact that not all of the high-paying jobs are fascinating, and not all of the really fun ones pay well. It's all about balance, so I'm going to share with you how I balance my mix of customers, which might help you, too.

What are the types of customer?

Whatever industry you're in, you tend to have a few types of customer:

Customers who send you a lot of work regularly (great, although try not to rely on just one or two of these, just in case, and sometimes they can get a bit demanding)

Customers who send you a bit of work irregularly (only keep these on if you really can slot them in as and when)

Customers who pay high rates (why? they may have set the rates for their industry and they're in a region with higher costs of living and pay rates for freelancers)

Customers who pay lower rates (why? you might have long-standing customers on a historical lower rate or offer discounts, as I do, for special groups of customers such as students, individuals and music journalists)

Customers who have fascinating work that's right up your street and relates to your interests

Customers who have dull work which nevertheless you can tackle

Customers who always need their work to be done at the last minute

Customers who send you stuff that's at the edge of your comfort zone – or outside it

These last two are the ones who you really do need to have as few of as possible.

As I said, in an ideal world, you would have customers with loads of fascinating work who pay high rates. But that's not always going to happen, so it's a matter of …

BALANCE.

Isn't it always, though?

Boulders, pebbles, sand

Time management gurus make use of the **boulders, pebbles and sand metaphor** when talking about how to fit your tasks into your day. The idea is that you slot the big jobs (the boulders) in first, then you can fit pebbles (smaller jobs) in around them, and fill up the gaps with sand (I usually see the sand as being my admin tasks). So, if I have a big transcription that must be done by tomorrow and will take three hours, I will plan to do that in the afternoon, and slot a couple of small editing jobs around it.

It's the same with customer types.

It would be great if you loved *loved* LOVED all of your projects, but some of them are still going to be more interesting than others. To take some aspects of my work as an example (but, as I said, this works for all industries) …

- **Localisation** is my most lucrative work but it's often fairly repetitive marketing or web texts. It also often uses specialised software that can be quite tricky to work with.
- Working with **translators** is a specialised job and so my rates are higher than for native English editing. The texts I get from my translators and agencies are varied and often interesting.
- I have a particular **transcription client** who pays great rates and has interesting tapes to send me. Their work is less regular, but still interesting.
- I love transcribing for **music journalists**. Music is an obsession of mine and I love both hearing all the bits that don't make it into the articles and seeing how the articles are written up from the tapes I've transcribed. But I do charge these clients less than my corporate transcription rates, because they're usually freelancers like me. These are very, very rarely uninteresting, even if I'm not a big fan of the music style. Or if it's Justin Bieber.
- **Student work** can be interesting but I charge a lower rate than for corporate editing and it can be very tricky and time-consuming, because it typically involves quite a lot of emailing back and forth. I used to work on Master's coaching, but found that it was difficult to commit to small bits of work coming at short notice over a long period of time.

How I balance my customers out

To maintain the analogy of the boulders and pebbles, this is how I manage this customer base:

Boulders have to be **regulars with the more lucrative end of the work**. I have kept down my number of localisation clients – I could do just localisation, but it would be a bit same-y and I would end up relying on very few, large clients, which is something I avoid. So: regular localisation clients, regular translator clients and at the moment a large regular transcription client are the boulders of my client base.

Rocks are my **music journalists** (see what I did there?). The work is fun, the clients are lovely, and I get more return on investment than just the money. But I have to be careful not to take on too many of these, because I do not make as much per hour and I am in this job to make a living. I do let the odd rock crash into my personal time, because these clients are often on odd schedules. But I encourage them to book me as far in advance as they can, and they do pay extra for urgent work.

Pebbles – **student work** and the occasional one-off **fiction or non-fiction book** referral from a regular customer. I'm afraid I am more likely to take on a referral than somebody out of the blue these days – but I will always refer on anyone who I can't take on. I already pass on all Master's students to one of three colleagues who have the time and attention they need. Also in this category come the few clients I still have who send small projects regularly – if you have few enough of these, you can slot them in around the rocks and boulders. I have one client who sends me middle-sized projects but with lovely long deadlines – work I can break into pebbles and pour around the bigger jobs.

Sand of **administration** – my monthly invoicing session is a boulder, but because each job is small, I can slot a few email replies or jotting down some blog post ideas among all of these.

It's all about the balance

When it comes down to it, it's all about **balance and return on investment** (which doesn't take a solely monetary form: see the next section). This is how I balance my own work:

- I could do just localisation all day every day, and push for more of that work, but it would be a bit repetitive and I could run the risk of only working with a few, large clients, which leaves me a bit exposed.
- I could just work with translators and translation agencies, but I'd only really be editing then and I like the variety of my other work.
- I could just work with music journalists and have a whale of a time listening to all sorts and picking up on new band to like. But the work can fluctuate madly so it would be unreliable as a steady source of income. And I'd probably get RSI.
- I could just work with students and self-publishing novelists, but I wouldn't make enough to live on doing that full time, and again, I'd just be editing all day, every day.

By balancing all of these different customers (and you can do the same, whether you're a roofer with a mix of full roofs, porches and repair jobs; or a decorator doing whole houses, front doors and window screens; or a graphic designer creating adverts, logos and cartoons), I get variety, optimise my income and have fun!

When should I say no?

When you work for yourself, especially when you're starting out, it's all too easy to say "Yes, please!" to every job that comes your way. But it's a good idea to start saying "No, thank you" early on – not to everything, but to certain kinds of job. What you say no to depends on where you are in your career and what your schedule's looking like, but here are my top jobs to turn down …

Note, with all of these, it's often OK to say "yes" to one of the kind of job, just to see. But you'll probably find yourself saying no later on!

What to say no to early in your career

Working for free. Caveat. If someone asks you to work for free AND they are an influencer who is likely to recommend you on AND they agree to give you a reference AND you've got time to do it without turning down paid work, then go for it.

Doing something you feel uncomfortable about. It's good to push yourself into new areas, but that's not what I'm talking about here. I'm talking about anything on the wrong side of your ethical line. Just because you're starting out and are a bit desperate for work doesn't mean that you should go against your own principles.

Doing something way outside your normal line of work. I think it's a good idea to consolidate your reputation in one area and then branch out from there. By all means try something out, but if you don't like doing it or it doesn't fit, say no next time.

Working again with rude, pushy or unreliable clients. If someone's rude to you on the first job you do for them, or they don't pay when they say they will, it's OK to say no next time. You are worth more than that, and a difficult client now will always be a difficult client. Demanding, fine; rude and pushy, not fine. Don't let your self-worth get undermined before you get started.

What to say no to at the mature stage of your business

Anything that will overload you. If you find yourself saying, "Well, I could fit this in if I don't sleep on Thursday night" or "Well, if person x doesn't send me their chapter on time I could do this", it's probably time to say no and recommend someone else.

Small jobs that don't look like they'll turn into regular customers. Cruel but true – the smaller the job, the more noise to signal (admin to work) there will be. Pass the little ones on to your newer colleagues who need to build up their portfolio.

Discounts. You should be experienced enough to stand by your pricing. You will have discounts worked out for various sectors but at this stage, you shouldn't be in the business of buying work, and that's what this is doing. If your prices are fair, don't offer discounts except in exceptional circumstances.

Regular clients who don't match your needs. Maybe they don't pay well / on time or are difficult to deal with or have time scales that don't match your own – sometimes it's time to say goodbye and pass them on to another recommended practitioner.

What to say no to throughout your career

Any job with 'danger' flags. To me, the main one here is "We've been through a lot of people and haven't found the right partner yet" or "I've had problems with my previous editor / roofer / plumber". By all means, check what the problem was. There are bad examples of every job out there, and you can be the one to fix the problem. However, if there's an on-going pattern of problems, or they can't be specific about what went wrong last time, my advice is to avoid.

Any job where you need to spend a lot of time learning a new system or skill UNLESS you really do have the time to do that and it's going to be useful for lots of work in the future. I have had to turn down jobs that involve learning a new kind of translation software recently – I knew I had time to do the work, but not to learn the software. Best to tell the client up front!

Any job that goes against your moral code. However much of a dip or a bad patch you're going through, however much it comes from a current client, if you feel uncomfortable doing it, don't do it. (I had that situation a little while ago – I said no, I said why, they were fine with it and are still working with me.)

A client with unrealistic expectations. If someone expects me to write their book from their notes in a small space of time but call it (and charge for) proofreading services, or thinks I can transcribe 10 hours of tape in 12 hours, they are likely to be turned down. Setting and managing expectations is a whole other post, of course …

It's great to say yes and it's great to be busy – but it's also vital to be able to say no and to be able to keep your busyness to a decent level. If you're going through a dip in your mature business, go back to those early stage noes, and keep firm about them!

Oh, and although I do say no fairly regularly, I do almost always refer the prospect on to a recommended colleague who might have the time / capacity / skills to help them. If you do the same, it's a win-win-win – the client will come away with a great impression of you, your colleague will have a new prospect, and you will feel reassured that you've done the right thing by not leaving them without any support.

Investing in your business

You can't do anything in life without a bit of investment:

- It's hard to find a life partner if you don't go out there meeting people (or advertising, or looking online …)
- You can't have certain careers without training for them – fancy being a roofer but haven't learned how to use ladders properly? Or a plumber with no knowledge of sewage and water supply?
- You can't write the Next Great Novel without learning something about your craft
- You can't publish the Next Great Novel without having it edited and proofread
- You can't live in a warm and dry house that you own without doing some maintenance
- You can't run a successful business without investing in yourself and the business

In this section, I'm going to talk about how you know when it's worth investing, how to work out your return on investment, share what's been worth it for me, personally (with a few other people's input) and, finally, I'm going to talk about a very specific investment: your website.

How do I know when it's worth investing?

You want to invest in something, but how do you know when it's worth it? Is it worth laying out a sum upfront, or is it always better to save first? In this chapter, I reflect on some purchases I've made which have been worth it (and some that haven't), and discuss how you tell in advance if a purchase is going to be worthwhile.

How do you tell whether an investment is worth it?

Investments for a small business can be broken down into:

- Outsourcing (paying other people to take on tasks you might do in-house)
- Products, materials and services
- Training

Is it worth outsourcing this task?

I've developed some simple rules about how to tell when it's time to outsource a task to do with your business:

- If you're rubbish at doing something and someone else is good at it, outsource it to them (even if you've got the time to do it yourself or it's going to cost you more per hour)
- If the time it will take you costs more in your worth per hour than it would cost to pay someone else to do it, outsource it. For example, if transcribing your interview will take you 6 hours and you're worth £40 an hour (£240) – better to send it to someone who can do it for you for £120.

This links into a couple that are about time:

- If it's going to take you 6 hours to do but someone else 3 hours to do, outsource it
- If it's going to take you 6 hours to do and someone else 6 hours to do, but you don't have 6 hours free, outsource it

But you can add in some other factors, too, such as the boredom factor:

- If you're perfectly able to do the task and it would cost more to have someone else do it, but it bores you to tears and you never get round to doing it until it turns into an unholy mess, outsource it.

This last one is why I decided to hire an accountant to do my accounts and my bank reconciliation.

Is it worth buying this product or service or these materials?

What about investing in products and services? These are my rules:

- If it will make my work more quick or more efficient – consider buying it
- If it will make my records more secure – consider buying it
- If it will advertise my services to my core market – consider buying it (for a year on a trial)
- If it costs under £100 – go for it

Points two and four combined to make me buy an external back-up drive and the professional version of my transcription management software.

Points three and four combined to make me sign up for membership to one membership jobs service which I've stayed with, and other sites and associations, which I have trialled and haven't stayed with (see the next section on working out your Return on Investment).

Of course the £100 level is arbitrary: I didn't select it consciously, I've just noticed that it's the level I'm comfortable with.

I don't use materials in my editing business but, if you do, the golden rule has to be:

Will the price of the item you're making be higher than the cost of the materials? If not: find cheaper materials or adjust your prices within sensible limits

Is it worth buying this training course?

And finally, training:

- Is the training run by an accredited provider that is respected in my industry?
- Does it train me on something I will use in my everyday work life?
- Will it add a skill to my portfolio that I
  - know there is a market for
  - will enjoy doing
  - have got time to commit to fully once I'm trained up?

Point two helped me decide not to take the training provided by a well-known and respected association, because they are all about editing on paper and I have done only one job on paper in five years.

And the last item is why I decided NOT to pursue training in the art of indexing. Yes, there's a market for it; yes, I would enjoy doing it; but no, I have a full roster of valued clients at the moment. If I was to take on indexing work, something would have to give: either my evenings and weekends, which I have pretty well reclaimed from Libro, or one or more of my current customers. I wasn't ready for either of those scenarios, so let it go.

Do I invest in advance or arrears?

This is a tricky one. I faced it myself recently with my first careers book, *How I Survived my First Year of Full-Time Self-Employment: Going it Alone at 40.*[11]

---

[11] http://librofulltime.wordpress.com/e-book-going-it-alone-at-40/

I really wanted to publish a print version of my e-book. I got some quotes for producing the back and spine cover art and wording, and for producing it as print-on-demand and fulfilling orders placed via the online bookshops. I would be able to buy copies for myself and sell them at events. I'd also have a physical book with my name on.

I was always adamant that the book needed to pay its way, i.e. I wouldn't do new or paid-for initiatives until the book had actually brought in the money to pay for it. Ignoring the hours I had put into writing and promoting the book so far, I would need to sell approximately five times as many e-copies as I had already to pay for the setup, design and print-on-demand service (the fulfilment cost comes out of the profit on each copy).

The figures indicated that I would make at least twice the profit on each print copy that I sell as I do on the e-books.

Should I wait until I'd made that money to go ahead? Should I wait until I'd made half of it and then risk the other half, assuming it would take me half as many books sold in print to get the investment back? Did I do it right away and hope I sold 2.5 times the number of books in print that I'd sold in electronic form to pay myself back?

Before, I had always waited until I had the money put aside before I bought something – I didn't invest in my new PC and laptop until my Libro business had been going for a couple of years and I had the money in the bank. But I was eager to get those print copies out there …

In the end, what I decided to do was invest a small amount of money in having the cover artwork redone and publish it in print form myself using CreateSpace on Amazon. I had the time to invest over Christmas, and this saved the money I would have spent. If it goes either really well or really badly, I'll invest in the professional service once I've sold a few more copies. And I can identify with

47

and support my clients when they go through this experience, from my own experience, too.

Working out my return on investment

In the previous section, I talked about how you work out if an investment is worth making. Now I'm going to look at how you work out what the ROI (Return on Investment) is for something you've bought.

What is Return on Investment?

Return on Investment (ROI) is what you get out of something as compared to what you put into it. A straightforward example is if you invest in some stocks and shares. If you put in £10,000 and get £11,000 back, that's a good ROI. If you put in £10,000 and get back £8,000, not so good.

It's not quite that simple if you're looking at your own investments, though.

Time / money / effort

Investments and their returns can be subdivided into several categories, for example, time, money and effort.

Investment:

Time: You might invest your time in learning a new skill or trying out a new tool, or writing your web text yourself.

Money: Lots of products and services and memberships cost money to buy. If you're bartering there is still a 'cost' involved, even if you're paying your proofreader in falafels!

Effort: I'm including emotional/psychological factors here. You might put a lot of yourself into going out networking if you're shy and would rather stay at home. Chasing late invoices can be full of effort if you hate hassling people for money. Working part time and running your business part time can involve a huge emotional and psychological investment, as can building relationships with your clients.

Returns on Investment:

Time: Do you save your time by using a new product or by outsourcing? Your time is also money, of course, but there is only so much time in the day, or week, or month, and you should really be concentrating on doing the core tasks that only you can do, whether that's making your jewellery, editing novels or selling widgets.

Money: If you streamline your production line with a new machine so you can make and sell more items per day, or get your invoices paid on time and improve your cash flow, or you buy a tool that makes your hand-made cards look more professional, then whatever you've done has saved you money, or made you more money.

Effort: If you hate doing something and you can pay someone to do it for you, or you want to branch out into a new area of work that you find attractive and interesting but need to do a course to get into it, or, indeed, you're tired of the day job and know that by working hard on your business you can move away from it and gain a more free and flexible lifestyle, then those all save you effort or bring you an emotional gain in the long term.

These factors can inter-relate, so you might get something like this:

- I spend MONEY on an accountant and she saves me MONEY in terms of the tax I pay
- I spend TIME setting up automated invoicing systems and save myself TIME every month when I run my invoices
- I put EFFORT into networking and save EFFORT in getting new clients in other ways I don't like to use, like cold-calling
- I spend MONEY on an accountant and she saves me time working on my accounts

- I spend TIME setting up automated invoicing systems and make more MONEY because I'm more efficient, and save EFFORT tracking down invoices and chasing up late payers

And of course, you can have negative or neutral returns on investment, too:

- I spent MONEY on paying to advertise on this website, but I've never directly made any MONEY from it. (Referrals can be tricky to work out as people sometimes see your name a few times before they buy, but if you pay for membership or an ad you should be able to see some direct worth coming from it.)
- I invested lots of TIME writing my blog but no one looks at it so I can't be making any MONEY from it and, if no one reads it and I never get any comments, I don't get any emotional (EFFORT) output either
- I made MONEY making these rip-off teddy bears but I feel awful that I went against my principles (EFFORT)

You get the idea.

So, is it worth it?

An investment, whether it's in a product, a service or something less tangible, is only worth it if you get more out of it than you put in.

This can be very subjective. If you hate doing your bank reconciliation, you might be happy spending more on an accountant to do it for you than your friend, who quite likes doing it. If you join a professional association but get no business, kudos, support or fun through it, then it's not worth paying those fees next year – but that can be very different for your colleague at a different stage of her career, as we will see.

So, it's a question of sitting down and looking at what you've bought, and working out whether the return on investment, in terms of money, time or less tangible factors is worth it. You can do this in advance, too, for example "I need a new computer, it will cost me money but save me time recovering from crashes and increase my income as I can do more work more efficiently", but you MUST also do this in arrears, rather than spend-spend-spend and never tot up the benefits.

Next, I'll be talking about the investments I (and some other people) have made, which have been worth it and which have not.

What's been worth it for me?

I've talked about how to tell if a product, service or outsourcing is worth it for your business and looked at Return on Investment, and how both the investment and the return can take the form of money, time or effort spent or saved. Now I'm going to share some examples of what investments have worked for me – and for some other people, too.

Investing in hardware and software

In terms of hardware, I've mainly spent money on these three:

New PC – definitely worth it in terms of speed and reliability. My current one doesn't fall over if I try to look at a whole PhD thesis in one go.

New laptop – definitely NOT worth it. I could see myself working in cafes with a coffee —but of course the kind of work I do doesn't go well with a noisy environment. Besides, I can't transcribe on a laptop keyboard, and find a trackpad tricky for editing. In addition, I spent extra getting a giant laptop with a separate numeric keypad, which means it's massive and heavy and hard to lug around.

External hard drive – definitely worth it. I spent under £100 and it automatically backs up all of my files every day.

My editor colleague, Laura Ripper,[12] wishes she'd thought more about her printer: "What I wish I had spent more money on, in hindsight, is a printer that will take several sheets at a time for photocopying. I hate standing over it feeding in one sheet at a time!"

---

[12] http://www.linkedin.com/pub/laura-ripper/26/7b1/714

I'm glad that we invested in a printer / scanner / copier as most of the printing I do nowadays is contracts and forms, which I invariably have to sign, scan and return to the client.

In terms of software, it boils down to:

Microsoft Office 2007 then 2010 then 2013 (the Small Business or equivalent editions) – must-have items. My clients use all sorts of ancient versions of Word, so I keep both 2007 and 2010 on my machine and at the moment am using 2013 as a learning tool for myself, blogging about the differences and features that I find.

Transcription management software – I have the paid version of the software I use (if you're interested, you can read a full article on this[13]) . It saves me time, and so makes me more money, by allowing me to work with many different tape formats and manipulate tapes using the function keys.

Invoicing and time management software – I did download a free time tracker but got so obsessed with my percentage of productive time that I became less productive! I use a simple invoice template that I designed myself, and add all a client's jobs on to their monthly invoice as I do them through the month.

Financial management software – I use my accountant's online system to record my bank reconciliation information.

Investing in other office equipment and reference materials

I am lucky in that my partner invested in a very expensive, posh office chair when he ran his own business. I've inherited that, and it's very comfortable. If you use a laptop a great deal, here's a nifty tip from Laura: "My laptop stand from IKEA[14] has meant I can

---

[13] http://libroediting.com/2013/03/27/working-as-a-professional-transcriber/
[14] http://www.ikea.com/gb/en/catalog/products/60150176/

actually sit at my desk all day if necessary without feeling like my wrists, neck or fingers are going to drop off. It was less than a fiver and was definitely worth the money!"

I'm very glad that I've invested in a range of reference books. I update the basic ones whenever there's a new edition, and I've also bought more on Plain English and international Englishes as I've gone along. I like using paper copies, having them there in front of me, and they save me from getting things wrong!

Investing in memberships and training

I'm going to present two different points of view on industry-related memberships here. Please bear in mind that these are about different people at different stages in their career. It might make you think, though.

I'm an established editor who also works in lots of other different fields, has clients around the world who tend to be translation agencies, translators, marketing companies and individual writers rather than publishers. I have decades of experience and lots of testimonials, and I'm busy enough that I can be very choosy about taking on new clients. I also work predominantly on electronic documents.

This does not make me too arrogant to join industry-based associations. I did try it, but I found that, while they're excellent for new editors, and provide training courses, forums and advice, most of the training is around paper-based editing for publishers, something that I very, very rarely do. For me, personally, it's not worth the effort, time and money to achieve qualifications in an area in which I don't actually work in order to progress my membership. But this is a very personal decision. However, Laura Ripper told me how useful she finds her membership of the Society For Editors and Proofreaders[15]: "It means I can attend my local SfEP group, so that's one way of meeting other freelancers and sharing ideas and information. It also gives me access to online forums like the Marketplace where members can post jobs they're too busy to do, and I've got a couple of jobs through that. You also get discounts on SfEP training if you're an associate or member. At the moment I'm only an associate, which isn't as good for marketing as I can't appear in the public directory, but after doing more training I'll upgrade. Oh and there's also the reassurance aspect for clients. I don't blog, so, especially before I got any testimonials, I felt that being able to use the SfEP logo (I checked this was OK) and say I am an associate would reassure potential clients that I'm professional in my work."

Other professional organisations do exist, in editing and in other professions, of course. But it's always worth reviewing, when you've paid for that first year, what you got out of it in terms of support, jobs or referrals.

On the other hand, one membership that has worked well for me is my local business association. I pay a minimal sum, have an advert in their directory, and get to go to breakfast get-togethers: at just one meeting, I met a carpenter, a financial advisor and a solar panel installer all of whom I will be in touch with later!

With regard to training, if it's tailored to what you need and focused on your business, it can bring a great return. I'm largely self-taught but I have an English degree including a lot of Linguistics behind me, plus jobs working on dictionary editing and in marketing. I discussed my choice NOT to take an indexing course earlier, and I keep up my professional knowledge by reading blogs, checking the new editions of textbooks and participating in forums.

Sarah Bartlett[16] has had this good experience: "I have come to value one-to-one training from trusted freelancers in their area of expertise

---

[15] http://www.sfep.org.uk/

with the training tailored to my needs. That's the best money I've spent this year so far and I intend to do it again. It's brilliant value for money."

Investing in marketing and advertising

This splits down into two sections: marketing and advertising that you put money into, and marketing and advertising that you put time and effort into.

Paid-for advertising

The two main things in terms of advertising that have done it for me have been:

- Very local and specific advertising – early on in my career, I advertised my student proofreading services in the University staff magazine. I ran the ad for a year at a cost of £120 and made that back many times over.
- Thanks to my friend, Sian, I bought membership of proz.com, which is mainly for translators, because I work editing people's translations and people also go there looking for localisers and transcribers. That costs around £50 a year, and for that, your details are put in front of prospective clients when they put forward a particular job. I have made this money back many, many times over; probably a hundred-fold each year. Definitely worth it.

I have joined some free listings sites and get a few enquiries from them, but not enough to justify paying for enhanced listings. Some listings companies charge a fortune; others, like the thebestof[17] range in the UK can be useful if you have a very local client catchment area.

---

[16] http://bartletteditorial.com/
[17] http://www.thebestof.co.uk/

Marketing-wise, I tend to use Vistaprint for business cards and postcards. While many people dislike Vistaprint, I design my materials carefully so they are attractive, and pay to not have "vistaprint.com" on the back. People generally like them, and I do too – but I don't give out millions of cards, so it is worth going to a more specialised designer if you're giving them out all of the time.

Julia Dickson from Patricks Pieces[18] has a good point here: "I quite like my Vistaprint cards but that's probably because I use their plain template and import my images, that way I don't have the same motif as everyone else."

If you need to call attention to yourself at craft fairs and around and about, here are some great investments people have made:

Sarah Goode from jewellery company, Pookledo[19] says, "I've invested in good display units to make everything look coherent". And Hev Bushnell from Hev's Happy Hounds[20] explains an interesting marketing concept: "My car. I covered it in pawprint vinyls and also paid to have lettering on the back. I also invested in car business card holders. Since doing the car, my business has boomed!"

Also worth paying for:

- Professional photographs. I was lucky and called in some social capital here (i.e. got a friend to do it – but he is a professional photographer)
- Website – If you're not an expert, it's far better to have a website designed and written for you than to link to a woeful attempt full of 1990s design and typos. On investing in a website in particular, see the next section.

---

[18] http://www.facebook.com/PatricksPieces
[19] http://www.pookledo.com/
[20] http://www.hevshappyhounds.webeden.co.uk/

Marketing using your own efforts

I've invested time and effort, but not money (unless you count the money I could have made if I wasn't doing these things) in the following:

- Website(s) and blog – these maintain and grow my reputation, bring people to me, and allow me to share what I do as well as help people. They take a long time to put together but showcase my writing and I do enjoy doing it, too.
- Guest blog posts – I've been placing these more often recently, to help to promote my books. It's a good way to get link backs to your own website / blog and to get your name known. I offer guest spots on my blogs, too, of course.
- Commenting on other blogs – comments I've made on colleagues' and other writers' and business peoples' blogs send people to my own sites even years later, and you never know what someone might be looking for
- Social media – having a presence on Facebook and Twitter has definitely got me clients. All of my music journalist clients have come out of one response to a tweet from someone looking for a transcriber, taking me on and recommending me to her colleagues (thanks, Jude![21])

However, paid work comes first and these efforts fit around it.

Investing in networking

I looked at the big, nationwide networking groups, and they can be good for some people. Personally, I find that it's hard to explain what I do in 40 seconds at breakfast, and I'm not able to bring in referrals for other people to every monthly meeting (to squish

---

[21] http://www.juderogers.com/

together what the two main big organisations do). I do however go to more informal networking groups, and I've made friends, got advice and support and made contacts that have led to jobs at the Social Media Cafe[22] in Birmingham.

Looking at networking in a wider sense, I gain great support, laughs, help and a feeling of being part of a group of peers from my editor colleagues on Facebook and in person, and other business colleagues on Facebook, Twitter and LinkedIn.

Investing in outsourcing

This is a work in progress. As I have already mentioned, I have taken on an accountancy firm to do my bank reconciliation, provide me with certified accounts and prepare my tax return. I feel that the financial cost has been outweighed by the peace of mind and time saved messing around balancing my books!

---

[22] http://birminghamsmc.com/

Investing in a website – is it worth it?

In my networking adventures, I come across quite a few people who don't have a website. To be honest, I'm a bit shocked when this happens. Unless you've got a constant set of clients, with new ones on the horizon to fill in any gaps if you lose one, then you'll want to be findable.

When you think about getting the roof done, or finding a cleaner, or sourcing flowers for an event, or buying a product, where do you look?

Online.

Even if you look for a tradesperson on a Yellow Pages style website, I bet you like to have a URL to click through to, to look at their details. Right?

If you don't have a website, even a single page with your name / company name and information about yourself, then what will people find when they search for you?

How do people search for companies, products or services?

People come to my website in one of four ways:

- They search for my name
- They search for my company name
- They search for something that I do

They search for the answer to a question ("is it *en route* or *on route*?" "How do I repeat the header row of a Word document on every page?")

This is what would happen if I didn't have a website:

- If they search for my name, they'll find my Twitter or Facebook feed, or photos of me socially, or mention of me on forums. All fine, but they'd probably rather find either my Facebook or my company information in one place

- If they search for my company name, they will find my Facebook or Twitter feed, however, those mention and feed back to my website, as they're not enough in themselves to maintain interest and get me business
- If they search for something that I do, they'll find someone else's website and if they're looking for someone to do that work, they'll hire that someone else
- If they search for an answer to a question, someone else will answer it, and if they're looking for someone to work for them, they'll hire that someone else

This is what happens because I have a website:

- If they search for my name, they'll find my website and my other feeds, which all link together. They'll find out what I do and if they want to talk about work, they can contact me
- If they search for my company name, they'll find my website, find out what I do, and possibly hire me, getting in touch via my contact form
- If they search for something that I do, they'll find my website, find out that I do that, find references from people who I've done that for before, and possibly hire me – getting in touch via my contact form
- If they search for an answer to a question, if I can answer it, they'll find out that I know what I'm talking about, and note me for later or sign up to receive emails when I post, and might hire me in time, or ask me a question or engage with my blog

The bare minimum

As a bare minimum, you should have a page somewhere that includes:

- Your name
- Your company name (if it's different)
- A list of your services or products – make sure that you mention all of the forms of the things you do on that page (so I would include transcriber, transcription services, editor, editing, etc.)
- References from satisfied customers
- A way to get in touch with you – a contact form, a phone number (most people like to see this), an email address
- Professionally produced text – by which I really mean have someone check it for typos and spelling mistakes. Those will seriously undermine your reputation and send people running from your services – whatever they are

It's a good idea to have your company name in the URL for your website, but personally I don't hold it against small companies if they have the word blogspot or wordpress in their URL – you don't need to pay extra to have that if you don't want to.

You can use a Facebook page as your company web page, however I would hesitate to ONLY use something that changes so often and is as unpredictable as Facebook. A company Facebook page is better than nothing, however!

Optional extras

You can add these extras if you want and if they add value. If you find that you're getting a steady stream of enquiries via your simple website, and they turn into paying customers, then only add these items if you can see a clear value in doing so, rather than doing it out of vanity or because someone's persuaded you to buy their service:

- A URL that's just your company name – you will have to pay for this, probably renewing annually
- A professionally designed website – there are so many 'themes' on offer that look as good as professional websites.
- A blog – this is GREAT for driving people to your website and setting you up as an expert in your field. If you only do one of these things, write a simple blog
- Someone to write web text and blog posts for you
- Search Engine Optimisation – a professional can ensure that you're showing up in the search engines etc. But shop around – this can be expensive and there are lots of things you can do to SEO your site on your own (just have a little search engine search and see what you can find)
- A shopping cart and catalogue – very useful if you're producing craft items or any tangibles – but you can sign up to services like Etsy and eBay which will do this for you

The big caveat

It's really important to have a web presence so that people can find you.

It's really important to be super-vigilant, because unscrupulous companies prey on small businesses' lack of expertise in this area:

- Always ask around fellow small business owners or someone whose website you admire and see who they use
- If someone offers to make you top of the search engine results, ask what other sites they've worked on (always ask for references anyway) and do a search for yourself
- If someone offers to revolutionise your website and make you a millionaire overnight, they're probably over-selling. Ask for references
- If someone offers to build your website make sure – no, MAKE SURE – that you will be able to edit and update the

text and pictures on that website whenever you want to. Never hand over the full ownership of your site to another person such that you can't update it yourself.

If you haven't got a website, and you haven't got a steady stream of new and regular customers giving you a good income stream, I really do suggest that you get a website!

Blogging

Blogging is such an important part of business today. I can say with my hand on my heart that when I started blogging, it really did increase my visibility, made sure that I could be found on the various search engines, and brought me more customers. I can't quantify that, because I don't always know where people find me, but I do always ask, and "I searched on Google" is one of the common answers.

Blogging gives me these advantages:

- It positions me as an expert, giving people who might want to use my services added confidence that I know what I'm talking about
- It increases my visibility and search engine optimisation to attract people who might want to become clients OR who need the information I'm providing
- It allows me to share information and help people – I love receiving alerts about comments from people who have found what I have to say helpful
- It allows me to 'give back' by promoting other small businesses through a series of interview features and by quoting people's opinions on other business pieces
- It gives me an outlet for writing and a certain degree of creativity

I have to admit that I started blogging almost by accident, when I had an issue with a feature of Word (my comment boxes went tiny), struggled to find out how to sort it, and wrote myself some notes about how to resolve it, which I popped into a blog post so I could find it again. That post[23] is still one of my most popular, year on

---

[23] http://libroediting.com/2011/11/06/tiny-comment-boxes-in-word/

year, with over 16,000 views so far! I expanded that into a series on Word, which I still add to now, and then added in posts on pairs of words that get confused, business issues, and recently social media and blogging itself.

In this section you'll find out about ten reasons to write a blog (and ten reasons not to); the top ten blogging sins and how to avoid them; how to schedule blog posts and keep on writing them; how to host and place guest blog posts and why you should do this; and there are instructions in Appendix 2 on how to add a link to a blog post.

10 reasons to write a blog

Why should you write a blog? Why should you start writing a blog, and why should you continue writing a blog? Here are my top reasons why. I'm really looking at business blogging here, but the first one applies to everyone!

1. Because you want to

This reason covers both personal bloggers and business bloggers. You should start writing, and continue writing, a blog, because you want to. Forcing yourself to do something you don't want to do is no fun, and you should enjoy the time you spend designing and honing your blog and writing those entries. Whether you want to share holiday pictures or reviews of restaurants, or your professional expertise, do it because you want to.

2. You've got something interesting to talk about

There are so many interesting things to talk about. I often meet people running businesses where I have no idea of the nitty gritty of their everyday lives. How does a carpenter learn his trade? What does a freelance solicitor do, day to day? How many projects does a crafter have on the go at any one time, and how does a mobile hairdresser help their clients to choose a new hairstyle?

I have found that my posts on building my business struck a chord and interested many people, and I started blogging about Word hints and tips for myself really, but that has turned into a popular series, too. If you run a business, think about some of the behind the scenes things, some aspects of your knowledge that people might be interested to know. Don't worry about giving away your secrets – I might publish articles on Word headings and tables of contents, but I still get asked to do them by my clients!

Of course, it goes without saying that you shouldn't share personal details about your clients. But I think it's fine to talk about them if they're heavily disguised – or ask if they'd like to have a case study published with links back to their website!

3. It will set you up as an expert in your field

This is invaluable when you're building your reputation and your business. Don't see it as giving away information for free, think of it as sharing your expertise with the world. Once you start appearing in people's Google searches when they're trying to resolve a problem, they'll be more likely to come to you for help when they need your services. If you can offer a back catalogue of useful, targeted advice on your blog when you're negotiating with a new prospect, they will see that you can walk the walk as well as talk the talk.

This may not lead to direct sales – but I've often seen my blog posts shared among other people and organisations in my field. Keep your name in front of them as well as prospects, and you never know where the next recommendation and job might come from!

4. It will attract people to your website

This links in to the above point. The more content you have on your website which is packed full of keywords and language to do with your business, the more findable it is in the search engines. The more people find information that is useful to them and engages them, the more time they will spend on your website. The more time people spend on your website, or the more repeat visits they make, or the fact that they've signed up for your RSS feed and get regular updates into the RSS* reader or email inbox, the more likely they are to remember your name and your products or services when they, or a contact, need them. (If you're not sure what RSS stands for, have a look at the note at the end of this chapter.)

More website visitors does not directly lead to more sales in a quantifiable relationship. But as long as you do show genuine expertise and a willingness to engage with your audience, you will build your exposure, get more visitors to your site, and this will help you to become better known and gain more sales.

5. It will build your platform

Your platform is the group of people who are engaged with you in whatever way – through personal connections, social media such as Twitter, Facebook and LinkedIn, through your email newsletter, through your blog – and who can then be 'leveraged' (horrible term) when you want to get the word out about something new that you're offering.

For example, if you're self-publishing a book, it's vital to have built a circle of connections before it comes out, so you have a guaranteed audience of at least a few people. If you start offering a new service, for example when I added transcription services to my proofreading and editing offering, it's useful to have people who you can tell, and who will then hopefully spread the word.

Having a blog builds your platform because it engages people's interest. It brings them to your website, it gets them reading your content regularly, and it encourages them to sign up for your RSS feed (see below), or to receive your posts by email as they're published. Once you have subscribers, you can get information out to that guaranteed audience when you need to. That's much harder if you only have a static website for them to visit.

6. Regularly updated content will boost your position in search engine search results

It's fairly common knowledge that the search engines like content that is regularly updated. This means that their complex, little-known and ever-changing algorithms will promote websites that are frequently updated above those that are static. Updating your blog once a week or more gives all of the content on your website a better chance of being found by potential contacts and clients, because it gives it a better chance of appearing in a higher position in the search results.

7. So will information crammed full of the keywords that are important in your industry

Keywords are vital for search engines, too. If you just write a set of keywords over and over again, the chances are that the search engines will pick up that it's not real content, and will not show it to searchers. But if you are writing well-crafted copy which includes a good sprinkling of keywords among the text, you will find yourself doing better in the search engine results.

I write natural text in my blog posts that is (hopefully) interesting and gives something to the reader – but I am also careful to include relevant keywords at a regular rate in the blog posts I write, which does improve my search engine optimisation no end (it's also good to get them into sub-headings and the blog title itself). SEO is a fairly dark art, but the more keywords you can sensibly insert into your content, the more the search engines will be happy to find and display your content to their users.

8. You want to engage with your readers / prospects / clients

Blogs are not a one-way conversation. Once your audience has built a bit, you will get comments, shares, etc. on your blog posts, and on the places where you promote them (I get almost as many comments on a Facebook post advertising a new blog post as on the post itself).

One of the golden rules of blogging is that you need to respond to your comments. Some bloggers are very good at this, some are not. I'm sure everyone's commented excitedly on a blog post, only to find their comment is effectively 'ignored', with no reply from the writer. I think that's quite rude, and I am likely to engage a lot less – or stop engaging – with bloggers who have a habit of not replying. Obviously, we all get times when we're away or too busy to reply that moment, but most blogging platforms alert users to replies, and you want to keep that feature switched on and engage with your audience, otherwise they will stop coming back. And those commenters might just be your friend Ali or your ex-colleague Steph, but every person who engages with your blog is a potential client or recommender.

9. You want to engage with other bloggers

There's nothing like blogging for building communities of like-minded people. Once you're blogging in a niche area, whether it be fiction writing, editing, ironing services or Sage, people who are interested in the same sorts of areas will start to follow your blog, comment on your posts and share what you're saying.

This is useful for a couple of reasons: firstly, it's always good to have colleagues. I've written elsewhere about how I treat other people in the same line of business as colleagues rather than competitors. Sometimes you need to have a moan or a chat or ask advice, and you might want to do this privately rather than publicly, which is where your network of colleagues can come in very handy. You can also read what they're saying, get new ideas, keep up to date, and slot into networks that offer mutually useful posts, services and applications.

Secondly, this may give you the opportunity to guest post on other people's blogs, and vice versa. We'll talk about sharing your content in other places next. But just to give you some examples, if I hadn't started blogging, I wouldn't have got to know many of the editors I now know who link to my blog articles, share them on social media, and act as a sounding-board when I need to talk things through. That's worth every hour of effort I put into my blog, to be honest!

10. You want to share your content in other places on the web

The good thing about your URLs and name appearing in places on the web that are not connected directly with you, your website and social media is, you guessed it: it boosts your position in search engine results. The more times your URL appears on a website that's on a solid standing itself and has followers and people talking about it, the more the search engines will consider your website to be appropriate to present in their search results listings.

These links to your content on other people's pages are called backlinks. You can secure these in a number of ways:

- Comment on someone else's blog post, including your URL
- Contribute when someone asks for examples, experiences or feedback, again making sure that your URL is included
- Write a guest blog post for someone – ensuring that the biography at the end includes all of your links

Now, you'll know if you've ever allowed comments on a website or blog that a lot of companies do this seemingly randomly, just to get their URL into other people's comments, and now you know why they do it. So do make sure that the content and comments you share are appropriate to the topic of the post on which you're commenting! But this is a great way to increase traffic to your website and blog.

So, there are 10 top reasons for writing a blog. Next up, 10 top reasons NOT to!

*What's this RSS stuff I keep talking about? RSS feeds are file formats that allow your regularly updated content to be collected and sent on to readers, usually involving them reading all of the blogs etc. that interest them using an RSS reader that accumulates them all in one place. This Wikipedia article[24] explains it all and examples of RSS readers include Feedly.[25] To find the RSS feed on a blog, look for the symbol at the beginning of this explanation.

---

[24] http://en.wikipedia.org/wiki/RSS
[25] http://www.feedly.com/

10 reasons not to write a blog

We've just looked at 10 reasons to write a blog. But what are the reasons for not writing a blog, or for taking an informed decision to stop writing one, even if you started?

This section, like the last, is mainly targeted at business bloggers. However, if you have a personal blog that you want to gain an audience, and maybe earn some money, from, these points will interest you, too.

So, what are the reasons NOT to write a blog, or to give up?

1. You are only doing it because someone told you that you should

I go on about blogging to people ALL THE TIME. I even did it when I was buying vegan food from a stall in Greenwich one weekend. But don't just do it because someone tells you to. OK, it's worth looking at the reasons why having a blog is good and making an informed decision, but if someone just tells you, "start writing a blog" and you do, it's not as likely that the habit will stick and it will be useful and fun.

2. You actually dislike doing it

So, you've started blogging and you've got into a routine, and then you realise that you're just dreading writing that next post. I'm going to talk later about slumps and maintaining momentum. But what I'm talking about here is hating it all the time, disliking putting fingers to keyboard and putting the thing together, resenting the time it takes up. If you don't enjoy doing it

- get someone else in your organisation to do it
- pay someone else to do it
- stop doing it entirely

3. You haven't got time to post regularly

If you have a personal blog and you're not worried about statistics and search engines, you can get away with blogging very irregularly, but if you are doing it so as to appear in search results and get more exposure for your business, you really do need to post regularly and reasonably frequently. I find that, for me, three posts a week are the sweet spot. When I do this, I get the most visits to the blog. It's worth noting that not all of those are long posts (my Troublesome Pairs certainly are not), but it's regularly updated content, full of relevant keywords and useful to different groups of readers.

Once a week is, I think, the minimum you can get away with and still gain value from the process. If you don't have the time to do this, again, consider outsourcing, or consider not doing it at all.

4. You're not organised to post regularly

Following on from the time issue, you do need to be organised enough to generate new content fairly regularly. Again, I'm going to talk about this in detail later, but you do need to plan what you're going to talk about, gather photographs and illustrations for the posts, organise yourself to sit down and write them, and then publicise the posts and deal with any comments that might ensue. If you fly by the seat of your pants, doing everything as and when, and find organisation in general to be a tricky thing, blogging for business might not be for you.

5. You're only in it to make money

You do read loads of posts about making money from your blog. And you can make money from your blog, for example by:

- Allowing adverts to appear on your blog (but be very careful with this and make sure you only allow adverts relevant to your readers or this will be a big turn-off. The best way to do this is through carefully selected product placement that matches with your content and readership)

- Hosting affiliate links on your blog so that readers can click a button or picture on your blog to be taken through to buy a product, while you get a percentage of all sales (this is notoriously difficult to make money from)
- Selling your blog to a publisher to make into a book (but not many people make money writing and selling books, and there's more to a blog-to-book than just bunging all your blog posts in one place – read this blog post if you want to know more about my direct experience of this[26])

It's not common to make money directly from your blog. It's hard to say how many page views you need per month to do well out of advertising, but recommendations start at 10,000 unique visitors per month. Not many publishers convert blogs into books outside the big ones we've all heard about. What my blog does is let people who may become customers know about me … but that's using your blog to build your business, not to make money per se. If you've read an article or been to a seminar about easy ways to make money online, be VERY careful what you sign up for and get into.

6. You are not interested in engaging with your readers

People who read blogs like to comment on them. People who comment on blogs like to see the blogger reply to these comments. I know that personally I've stopped reading and commenting on blogs when I'm never responded to, especially if I can see that the blogger never responds to any comments. This is actually one of my Top 10 Blogging Sins, too.

---

[26] http://libroediting.com/2013/06/12/an-editor-writes-10-lessons-i-learned-when-writing-my-own-book/

If you're not actually interested in having a conversation, in engaging with your readers, in replying to their comments, and you just find it a chore; if you just want to broadcast and don't want to engage in two-way conversation, I don't personally think that blogging is for you. You will lose readers as fast as you gain them, and it will never be personally or professionally fulfilling for you.

7. You are not interested in engaging with other bloggers

This is similar to point 6, but we're talking here about other people in the same line of business as you (whether that business be small business support, engineering or book reviewing). If you see other people blogging on a similar topic to you as rivals, and you want to set yourself apart and distance yourself from them, then you may not find blogging to be useful. You probably can't 'beat' the most successful blogger in your industry, and if you don't want to engage with them, share guest blog spots, link to their material and comment on each other's blogs, then it might be wise to disengage with the process.

8. You haven't got anything interesting to say

If you're boring yourself with your blog content, you will probably be boring your readers. If you're constantly scratching around for topics to write about, or covering the same ground time and again, consider scrapping either that series, if you have various topics you cover on your blog, or the whole thing. I used to post up an update about what I'd been doing at the beginning of each month. Although some readers said they enjoyed it, it was becoming very repetitive and boring to write. So I stopped and added something else in that slot on the blog.

Note: what you think isn't interesting might be to other people – it's always worth doing some market research. When I meet people like locksmiths, carpenters and electricians, I always tell them they should write a blog about their daily lives and the jobs they do (keeping their clients' confidentiality, of course) as many of us would find that sort of thing really interesting. I'm talking about when you're struggling for ideas and you're maybe not getting any positive feedback or a growing readership, and your blog becomes bogged down and repetitive. Have a rethink or ditch the blog!

9. Your blog isn't relevant to your target market

If you're blogging for business, your blog posts need to be relevant to your target market(s). For example, I blog about:

- Word tips and hints – because most of my clients and target market use Word
- Language tips and hints – because my business lies in improving written language
- Business tips and hints – because I've written a book about business and I am passionate about engaging with other businesses
- Blogging tips and hints – because I get asked about this a lot, and because of the business reason above, and because I noticed that I get searches coming through to my blog on that topic already, so I know people want to know about it

If you sell garages but blog about hairstyles, the people who read your blog are not likely to have a huge overlap with the people who are going to buy your services. If you have a book review blog and want to engage with mystery authors but only review romance, that's not going to engage your audience. There needs to be a big overlap between what you talk about on your blog and the people you want to attract to read it. Even 'the general public' has niches – people who like to read about fashion, or the work of an ambulance driver, or about low cholesterol eating.

10. Nobody is reading your blog, even after 6, 12, 18 months

It takes time to build a blog and its audience. Both of mine have grown over the months, pretty gradually. My book review blog wasn't growing its audience much for a while, and I did wonder whether to cancel it. I actually published a post asking if people found it interesting to see whether anyone was reading it! What I found out was that many people were reading it on blog aggregators, which don't show up on my statistics. So it was worth doing, but I also took steps to add value, beefing up my reviews, adding some more web pages to the blog, and importing a whole wodge of old reviews from another blogging service I used to use. My traffic improved and the blog was saved. But if you do that, and you change things and no one's looking, maybe it's time to consider other ways to market and raise awareness.

These are not necessarily ten reasons to stop blogging altogether. They certainly are reasons to stop, look at what you're doing, reconsider things and maybe tweak your posts, style, content or other aspects of your blog.

Top 10 blogging sins

We've talked about why to blog and why not to blog. Once you've committed to your blog, it can be a bit of a minefield. Here are the top ten blogging sins that I see over and over again, or hear other people complaining about. No one can be expected to know everything straight away, and we've probably all made at least one of these mistakes, so hopefully I'll help you to avoid the big, bad ones with this list.

1. Not having an RSS feed

Remember, RSS is a way to allow blog reader software to collect your content whenever it's updated and send it on to any of their readers who subscribe to your blog. Pop to the end of the "10 reasons to write a blog" chapter if you need more information.

If you look at the top of any page on my blog, you will see that I have an RSS feed logo in the top right-hand corner, a link in the right-hand menu bar, and I also offer a link to subscribe by email. All blogging software will have something in their settings that allows you to add this. If you don't add this link, it makes it that bit harder for people who want to subscribe to your blog. (They can usually put the URL in their reader software, but are they going to do that extra process? Not always.) Not having a button to use to do it quickly and easily can give the impression that you're not interested in people reading your blog. That's probably not true. But I've seen people get really cross about this and say that they're not going to look at a person's blog any more if they don't have this. I know … but if one person's saying it, how many are thinking it?

If you get stuck trying to add this button to your blog, the easiest way to find out how, is to Google your blogging software's name and "RSS feed button". You should find a YouTube video or set of instructions telling you how to do it.

2. Not updating your blog

If you set up a blog and you then don't update it, it won't help you to get more readers or to promote whatever it is you're promoting. Google and the other search engines thrive on updated, fresh content. If you don't update your blog regularly, it will fall further and further down the search rankings and no one will be able to find it. If you want to write a blog, commit to updating it regularly.

(The next section deals with scheduling and keeping active with your blog posts so, when you get to the end of this list, keep reading!)

3. Stealing content from other people

It's fine to 'reblog' other people's blog posts onto your own blog (where a snippet of the post appears on your page, with a link to the real thing). It's fine to link to other people's blog posts and tell other people about them. It's even fine to be inspired by another person's blog or content – one of my friends has started a questionnaire series a little like my Small Business Chat one but with an emphasis on marketing techniques: similar idea, different content, that's fine.

It's not fine to lift content wholesale from another person's blog or website. If you quote large amounts of text written by someone else, it's just the same as if you were using that in an article or essay – you need to reference where it came from and acknowledge the author. It's fine to talk about newspaper articles or reports in your blog and react to them, not fine to quote them verbatim, or quote people they have quoted, and not give the original source.

Never be tempted to take someone else's content for your blog post. At best, you won't get picked up by the search engines anyway (see below). At worst, you'll find yourself slapped with a lawsuit for plagiarism! And it's just not right.

4. Reusing content in exactly the same form

Say you've had a guest post on someone else's blog and you're really pleased with how it's turned out – so much so that you want to share it. So you post it in its entirety on your blog, too. Not a good idea.

All of the search engines, like Google, like to offer their users varied content. So if the same content appears in two places, both places won't come up in search results. Effectively, one of them will be invisible to search engines, therefore invisible to people searching for keywords that might lead them to that content.

To look at it from a different viewpoint, if you've published information in a guest post, the owner of the blog you're guesting on will want to be posting up original content, not things that can be found elsewhere. Some people actually specify that the content must be original in their guidelines for guest posters. How do you deal with this? Publish a snippet of the post on your blog, with a link to that post. Put some of your own text around it, then the search engines will find your post and your guest post, both of you will get found and viewed, and no one's copied anything. There are clever ways to deal with all of this in the coding behind your blog, but I'm guessing that most of us aren't the kind to deal with that level of complication – I'm certainly not!

5. Being rude or negative

I feel a bit of a hypocrite writing this, because this section is a little bit negative, but I'm genuinely trying to help people to avoid making common mistakes! In the same way, I tried to make sure that the chapter on "10 reasons not to write a blog" above talked about reasons for reviewing your blogging and content and making a positive decision. Whining and moaning and relentless negativity won't make your readers like you any more than they would like you in real life.

Being rude can get you views in the short term. But it's like those restaurants that people go to only because the waiters are desperately unfriendly. Fine for a laugh: but will they go back regularly for birthdays and anniversaries? Probably not. Even ranty blogs about politics or issues have to be constructive as well as rude!

If you want to have a rant or talk about a mistake you've made, try to vary and space out these posts, and make them as constructive as you can. We can all get a good blog post out of a bad experience (for example, an article that I wrote about my own experience as an editor being edited[27]) but make sure that you and your readers come away having learned something. The next section is all about managing your brand on social media, and this comes very strongly into that, too.

6. Posting inappropriate content

I don't just mean lurid or dirty pictures here. If you want to share information about your management courses, then blogging about your exercise classes won't get you the audience you want to buy your courses, unless you're doing some very clever keyword placement and making the articles valuable to both groups of readers.

I have to admit to having a laugh at funny spelling mistakes as much as the next person. However, I'm careful not to mock or talk about or post pictures on my blog, because a lot of the people I work with as an editor are unsure about their English and using it as a second, third, fourth language … and would be mortified if they thought people were laughing at them (I don't laugh at their English: I know I couldn't do half as well as my overseas clients if I was writing in my second language. Bong joor toot le world).

---

[27] http://libroediting.com/2013/02/13/on-being-edited/

7. Not giving your guest posters what they need

If someone takes the time to write a guest blog post for you to give you more, fresh content, bring their fans over to your website, give you a marketing opportunity, etc., etc., then you need to do certain things to make the experience a good one on all sides. Chief among these, and something I see people having issues with all the time, is making sure that you provide live links back to their website and whatever it is they're promoting, be it another website, their book on Amazon, or whatever. Formatting guest posts that have come through in an email or an attachment can be tricky, full stop. I recommend pasting the text into a Notepad file on your computer, then pasting it from there into your blog post (lots more on this below in the chapters on guest posting). But please make your guest blogger's links live so that your readers can visit them online!

8. Not letting people respond to your posts

I like responding to blog posts. We all like responding to blog posts. We like to feel it's a two-way conversation when we read something online, don't we? But I still come across blogs every day that either don't allow any comments at all, or make the commenting process so complex that people give up.

I have to say that the blogging software can be a culprit here. I can never seem to reply to Blogger posts, and WordPress itself can give the impression that you have to sign up to a WordPress account in order to comment on one of its blogs (you really don't, you just need to add your name and email address).

Enable comments, even if you moderate and check all of them for spam (most blogging platforms allow you to set the level of moderation, for example, I hand-moderate the first post by anyone, and am alerted to all new comments, so I can check they're not spammy or inappropriate). And listen to your readers – if you're getting complaints about how hard it is to reply to a post, have a look at your settings and see if you can make it easier. One of my blogging friends has a note whenever you go to comment with an email address to use if the process won't work – very helpful!

9. Not responding to comments

Allied to the above, if people take the time to reply to your blog, it's only polite to take a moment to respond to them. Some people who get a lot of comments will do a general reply mentioning all of the previous commenters with a sentence addressed to them, and that's of course fine. But I get a bit frustrated if I comment thoughtfully on a blog post and the author never responds. You don't have to do it immediately, but I try to do it within 24 hours, a couple of days at most.

Conversations on your blog can be one of the most interesting things about blogging – so get out there and engage with your readers!

10. Only advertising, never helping

Yes, I and other people have told you again and again that having a blog will help your business. That's true. But just blaring out adverts to your readers won't make them keep coming back. Imagine two blogs, both about plumbing:

One lists the different areas of plumbing the plumber can do, and has carefully inserted keywords to attract the search engines

One talks about the jobs the plumber has done this week, including how she solved a particularly tricky question. She sometimes posts a question and answer about a common type of issue, like changing the washer on a tap

Which blog will you go to once, to find a plumber? Which one will you bookmark and read, share and tell other people about? Which one will actually bring the plumber more business in the long term?

I give away quite a lot of free advice on my blog, but just because I tell people how to set up a table of contents doesn't mean that none of my clients ever ask me to do that now. On the contrary, seeing my expert advice, they trust that I can sort it out for them!

Scheduling blog posts, scheduling writing and keeping going

In this chapter, I'm going to talk about how frequently to blog, keeping going, and how to get down to writing those posts. Once again, it is primarily aimed at people who are blogging for their business, but the advice applies to anyone who wants to build the audience for their blog and needs help getting down to writing posts and sticking to blogging.

So that's everyone, right?

How often should I blog?

How often should you publish a blog post? Well, that's up to you to a certain extent. But if you're looking to appear high up in the search engine results and keep your readers happy, you should keep it regular.

Most advice that I've read suggests posting at least twice a week. This will keep your readers engaged, keep your content updated enough for the search engines to promote it up their lists, and get enough keywords and content out there to keep your statistics nice and busy.

Varying your blog posts

Even a book review blog could do with a bit of livening up every now and again. A good example is my friend Ali – she mainly posts long-format book reviews, but she also takes up general topics or talks about book-buying trips – which varies things for her readers and gives them something new every now and again.

I choose to vary things and give myself a structure by running series in different topics every week. I tend to publish a short Troublesome Pairs post about a pair of easily confused words or an article on blogging on a Monday, a Word tip or business post on a Wednesday, and I run a Business Chat or Chat Update each Saturday. I don't stick to this slavishly – for example I'll post on a Tuesday to avoid a bank holiday — but it helps me to structure things and means that there's something for everyone every week (I hope).

You don't have to just publish text pieces, either. I'm sticking to text for the moment, but you can include video and audio pieces as well.

If you want to get deeper into multimedia, I recommend that you read an article by Joanna Penn of The Creative Penn which has really good advice about when she schedules her text, audio and video content.[28] Her blog is really popular, with loads of comments and great search engine optimisation, and if you're planning on using different media, this would be a good plan to follow.

Including guest posts on your blog

Hosting guest posts (and having them on other people's blogs, too) is a great way to spark up interest and get reciprocal links and readers. And, it varies things a bit. I wouldn't personally have a guest post more than once every couple of weeks. (You can read more about the etiquette of guest blogging in the next two sections.)

How do I remember my ideas for blog posts?

If you're anything like me, you'll have ideas and inspirations for blog posts at the oddest moments. If I'm anywhere near my desk and PC, I pop into my WordPress platform and create a Draft blog post, sometimes with just a title, sometimes with a few jotted notes. If I'm learning something new (like turning footnotes into endnotes), I'll take screenshots as I go along, and save them to insert into a post on the subject. If I spot a picture I want to take, or have a document

---

[28] http://www.thecreativepenn.com/2011/02/09/content-marketing-for-authors-and-writers/

with a feature I want to use, I take a photo and email it to myself, or save the document in the relevant folder.

If I'm out and about, I use the note app on my phone to make a quick record of what I want to write about, or, if I'm feeling brave, I go into the WordPress app and create a draft from there!

How do I organise my images for my blog posts?

Because many of my blog posts are very screen shot based, and I always include some kind of image in my posts (looks good when sharing, attracts readers, etc.), I have a folder in my Windows Explorer called Blog posts. This has sub-folders for all of the blog posts I write, or plan on writing, so I can pop screen prints and pics into the appropriate folder and know they'll be there for later. I have a set of generic pictures in the Blog posts folder, too, that I can use as images at the top of posts. I prefer to use my own images to avoid copyright issues.

How do I get down to writing my blog?

Here's my secret: blogging SESSIONS.

You do not have to write your blog posts on the day you intend to publish them. You can write, save, and publish them, all in advance!

I've always got some draft posts on the go – either because I've had ideas (see above) and not yet written them up, or I'm part way through a series and I've planned the whole thing out. So when I can see at least a 90 minute slot in my schedule, I'll schedule in time to write blog posts.

I'll then bash through as many as I can, using my draft posts for inspiration and possibly already having pictures ready to go, either saved or inserted into the posts. Then I just need to write the text. In a good session I can get at least a week's worth of posts ready in one go.

I'm used to having to write because that's some of what I do in my job. If you have to wait for inspiration to strike before you write posts … just make sure that inspiration has plenty of room to keep going! Anyway, it's surprising what you can produce when you sit down and tell yourself that you have 90 minutes to generate a load of blog posts!

Scheduling the publication of blog posts

I would imagine that all blogging platforms have a scheduling feature. My experience is of WordPress: I can edit the Publish Immediately field to the right of my writing pane, and choose a date and time to publish the post (I also automatically post a link to Twitter, Facebook and LinkedIn. This means I can schedule a post to publish when I'm going to be away from my desk and the post will still be publicised).

If you don't know how to schedule blog posts on the platform you're using, Google your platform name plus something like "schedule blog posts" and you should be able to find instructions.

So, when I do a big writing session, I write the posts I want to write, then schedule them all in for the appropriate days. I can view just the posts I've scheduled to make sure there aren't any clashes, then I can get on with work or even go on holiday, knowing that my blog will be publishing when I'm away.

How do I make myself keep on blogging?

If you get stuck and don't post for a while, or don't feel like posting, don't panic! Here are some things you can consider doing:

- Have a think about why you're blogging and whether you do actually want to continue
- Have a little brainstorm and think of some ideas for blog posts – just jot them down and write them up later

- Get into a writing routine that suits you – whether that's posting once a day or having a weekly blogging afternoon
- Sign up for one of the various schemes that suggests something to post, or ask your friends or readers to make suggestions about what to write about
- Consider creating some themes – it's easier to come up with an idea for a Word tips post than an idea for 'a post'
- Don't beat yourself up. Look at other people's posts for inspiration. Ask for some guest bloggers. Review something you use in your work life. Write about something personal

Dealing with comments

Hopefully you will get a fair number of comments on your blog posts. You do need to schedule a little time to go through the comments regularly:

- Reply to positive or appropriate comments – no one likes to comment into a vacuum
- Set up comment moderation so that you, for example, see the first comment by a particular person and can approve or block it
- Monitor spam comments – spam should be trapped in a filter but can get through; if one gets into your moderation folder or onto the site, delete it and mark it as spam if you can (these are usually obvious by their URL being something to do with Ugg boots, handbags or other sales links)
- Monitor for abusive comments, delete or mark as spam (to highlight the commenter to their ISP or the blogging platform, don't engage with abusive commenters and remove their comments as soon as possible – make your blog a safe place for legitimate commenters
- Check the spam folder for legitimate comments and restore them

Guest posting 1: How to be the host(ess) with the most(est)

We know that placing your guest posts on other people's blogs and hosting other people's guest posts on your blog is A Good Thing: it increases traffic to both your website and theirs, gains you social capital, and gives you new, fresh and different content for your blog. (You can read more about that in the social media section coming up next.)

But how do you make sure that you do it right – for both you and your guest? Here are ten top tips to help you get the most out of hosting guest blog posts. If you only read and apply two of these, please make them numbers 7 and 8.

1. Know what you want

It's all very well deciding to welcome guest posts onto your blog, but what do you want to achieve? Do you want to show different angles on your line of business? Allow so-called competitors space to talk? Give your clients some publicity? Help other people in your geographical area? Start to formulate a policy rather than having a scattershot and random approach. This will help your readers to understand why you're hosting guest blog posts, and will help potential guests match their posts to your blog.

I accept guest posts on writing, especially on editors as writers and writers as editors. The more random ones I posted in the early days didn't get many hits, because they didn't really mesh with what I write about. The most popular have been ones that chime with my experiences, and the odd Troublesome Pair or Be Careful post that someone has written from the heart.

2. Know what you don't want

Once your blog has a certain reach, you'll find that people get in touch regularly wanting to place guest posts. Many of these seem almost completely random, with almost no (or absolutely no) relevance to my blog. I might give these people a second chance, but not often. I realised early on that there wasn't room on my blogs for random links to unconnected companies, or links to companies doing things that I didn't quite approve of – I get a lot of requests for 'guest posts' which are just ways for a company to place their client's URLs in popular places and build their SEO, and a good number for links to student proofreading companies that I wasn't entirely sure about.

3. Be clear on what you will and will not accept

Once you know what you want and don't want, you can narrow this down to what you will and will not accept. Most of the guest blog posts you publish will probably be suggested to you rather than commissioned, and it's up to you to say yes or no to these ideas. Personally, I will accept trial copies of relevant software or hardware and in my review I'll be clear if it is effectively a sponsored post, but I won't accept requests to place blatant ads. I might in future accept ads for products that I have reviewed, found good and am happy to recommend. I have got a few links that earn me an affiliate fee on my Links page, but I make it clear that I earn a fee from purchases coming from those clicks. Some people won't take any ads, some will take anything that pays. No matter what you choose to do, it's best to be clear about it.

So, once you know what will and won't accept, get clear about it. I have a Guest Post Guidelines page[29] to which I refer enquirers when they want to place a post with me.

---

[29] http://libroediting.com/terms-and-conditions/guest-blog-posts/

4. Commission guest posts

I get a lot of requests for guest posts, but I've also commissioned them (and been commissioned to write them too – I was asked to write one[30] after chatting about exercise with a fellow attendee at a networking event). Commissioning doesn't mean paying: it means asking someone if they'd like to contribute.

I have done this recently with a fellow editor who is less far along her business path than I am. She's got a specialism in which I'm interested, and fits with what I do, but isn't something I do, personally. So I've asked her to contribute a guest post on it, which will be interesting for my readers and get a link to her website on mine, too.

Another aspect of this is reciprocal posting. I did this recently with Tammy Salyer. I asked her to write a post on being an editor/writer,[31] and she then commissioned me to write about 10 top tips for fiction writing.[32] I've noticed a good flow of hits and referrals between the two posts – win-win for both of us!

5. Don't be afraid to give feedback

Once the post has been written and sent to me, rather than just publishing it as is or rejecting it wholesale, if there are aspects that I think could be changed, or I think the post needs major work, I will feed that information back to the poster. If there are minor spelling and grammar errors in Small Business Chats, I tend to change them silently (my initial instructions should make it clear that I'm likely to

---

[30] http://pbpersonaltrainingbrum.wordpress.com/2013/08/21/the-importance-of-keeping-fit-as-a-freelancer/
[31] http://libroediting.com/2013/06/05/living-with-the-dreaditor/
[32] http://tammysalyer.wordpress.com/2013/06/17/10-tips-for-fiction-writers-editor-spotlight-with-liz-broomfield/

do that), but if there's a more major content change, I will send a note to the poster before I publish (or reject).

6. Help people out

I try not to use guest posts just to give me me me more content, more hits, more interest. If I can give someone an opportunity to promote their book, service or specialism, AND it fits in with my blog and its readers, I'll offer them a guest post or accept their proposal. I do care about hits, but I also care about helping people and promoting things that are of value. That's why I've turned some of my own posts over to topics like Kiva[33] and the Soberistas,[34] and am happy to work in guest posts on topics that I feel are valuable.

7. Format the post

Most people will send their guest post to you in one of two ways: text in an email, or a Word document attached to that email.

Probably, like me, you usually write your own blog posts straight into the blogging interface you use – you hit New post and start typing. Fine, that's all new text and it should format OK. If you copy text straight from an email or Word document and dump it into your blog interface in a 'new post', you are likely to end up with a mess.

Word documents and most emailing programs contain all sorts of invisible formatting commands that will carry over into your blog post, running paragraphs together, putting it all in unfeasibly tiny print, and all sorts of other sins.

It's easy to avoid this. Copy the text that will form your blog post and paste it into a text-only editor – most PCs will have Notepad installed as standard, for example. Paste it in there and then copy it

---

[33] http://libroediting.com/2012/08/01/happy-birthday-libro/
[34] http://librofulltime.wordpress.com/2012/09/27/important-stuff-for-women/

and paste into your blog editor. Job done. You may have to reformat any links that the guest blogger has given you, but see the next point for how to work that one out.

8. Include links and an author biography

In my opinion, this is the most important one of the lot – and something that sadly I see going wrong quite a lot of the time.

If someone is decent enough to provide you with a guest blog post for your blog, be decent enough to tell your readers about them, and put in links to their product / service / book / cat pictures / whatever they want to promote – and that's LIVE LINKS, not just URLs that you can't click through.

I will share a good example with you[35] (I won't share a bad one, to save people's blushes). It includes an author bio with proper links that make sense and are in a different colour, so readers can find me and the book I wanted to promote easily.

It's great to reciprocate, but the effort someone has put in to writing a guest post for you will be simply thrown away if you don't provide links so that people can click through to them and their websites.

So make sure you ask your guest blogger for a quick biography and links to the things they want to promote (don't assume!), and then place the links in the article.

If you don't know how to create live links in your blog posts, read Appendix 2. Now.

---

[35] http://tammysalyer.wordpress.com/2013/06/17/10-tips-for-fiction-writers-editor-spotlight-with-liz-broomfield/

9. Share and promote

Once you've published your guest post, make sure that you share and promote it just like you do your own ones. It's nice to include the author's name and link in any posting you do on Facebook, Twitter, LinkedIn and Google+ etc.

This extends to telling the author that you've published the article and where they can find it – send them a link to the URL. And ask them to promote it, too. That way, you can leverage the social capital of both of you – or in simple terms, get more people to look and click. And that's really what guest posts are about!

10. Say thank you and feed back again

Once someone has been kind enough to provide you with a guest post, do say thank you publicly and privately. It's also nice to let them know how many hits the post has had – say in the first week. (You look at your stats for your posts, right?) You can also let them know how many click-throughs they got to their website or other resource. Also let them know if there are comments on the post that you think they should see or even reply to – not every guest will bookmark it and check obsessively for comments. But don't leave them to do all the responding – take part yourself, too. Again, the guest post that I wrote for Tammy Salyer[36] is a good example –both I and the host respond to the comments in turn.

---

[36] http://tammysalyer.wordpress.com/2013/06/17/10-tips-for-fiction-writers-editor-spotlight-with-liz-broomfield/

Guest posting 2: Being the perfect guest

Getting guest posts published on other people's blogs is generally considered to be A Good Idea. It can bring you new clicks, followers and even customers. But even if you're being commissioned to write a blog post for someone else, there are some unwritten rules that will help you to make it a success on both sides.

In this section, I share what makes a good guest blogger, from initial contact to thank yous, and share my ten top tips for being the perfect guest blog poster.

1. Do your homework

You've got a post you want to share and you think it's a good guest post. Before you even contact the host to ask them to post it, do your homework. Check whether they have a guest post policy: many busy bloggers will not even reply to you if you haven't looked and noted any guidelines. I will give people a second chance if I have time – but not always!

Presumably you know the blog because you've been reading it already. Have a think about who the audience is. What sort of posts does this person publish? How does your prospective guest post fit in with them?

2. Pick your hosts wisely

Have a think about whether this person welcomes guest posts. Are the posts they host on your topic or are they specific interviews or on other subjects? Is this someone you've engaged with on a long-term basis? Have you liked, shared, commented on their posts for a few months already? If they know your name and where your expertise lies, they are more likely to welcome your guest post.

Common advice is to only guest post on blogs that are more popular than your own. You can look at their Alexa[37] score and yours, for example, to see which is more popular. BUT, because part of my mission is to help other small businesses and colleagues, I'm happy to guest on smaller, newer blogs, to help to promote them as well as myself.

3. Demonstrate that you've done your homework

When pitching to place a blog post cold, or when replying to a commission, make sure that the host knows that you've had a look at their blog, that you're familiar with their style and content, that you have an idea who their readers are. Nothing annoys a blogger more than having a random person contact them saying "I have read your blog [on football] and I think this post [on nuclear physics] would fit really well, please post it and all my links as soon as possible". Even super-polite old me doesn't always reply to those ones!

4. Follow the guidelines

If a blog has guidelines for guest posts, as I and The Creative Penn[38] do, for example, then do follow them! (The Creative Penn ones are very detailed because it's a very popular blog with lots of guest posts, but as I said above, most people have them). In fact, if you can't find any published guidelines, ask the blogger if they have any specifications as to the ideal length, angle, etc. Make your piece match these as closely as possible.

5. Don't duplicate content

Google and other search engines do not like duplicated content. So make sure that any blog post you tout around is fresh, new content, not something that has appeared elsewhere or been pitched elsewhere. It's fine to pitch the same post to several potential hosts as long as you do it in series not in parallel, i.e. you wait for the first

---

[37] http://www.alexa.com/
[38] http://www.thecreativepenn.com/guestposting/

rejection, then try the next blogger. Also avoid doing this on your own blog (see point 9).

6. Help the host with the formatting

As we learnt in the last chapter, formatting text sent in by someone else can be a nightmare. If you really want to help your host, by all means write your post in Word so you can spell check it, etc., but then save as a plain text file with a .txt extension (drop down the Save as box when you're saving and choose "plain text .txt"). Your host can then open the file in a text editor and paste it into their blog editor.

You can always send a Word version as well, so they can see any bold or italics or other special formatting.

It goes without saying that you'll spell check your post and – if necessary – have it checked by your proofreader first, doesn't it?

7. Provide an author bio and links

To make it easy for your host, do provide a short author bio about yourself, and links to whatever it is you want to promote. I usually put together a few sentences on what I do and what I care about and then give the full URLs for the links, with an explanation of what they're linking to. Some hosts will put the links under the text, some will put them next to the text, all should make them live.

8. Accept feedback and give feedback

Many bloggers who accept guest posts will want to tweak your article a little to make sure it fits their guidelines, style and readership. Please do accept this graciously – you're playing round someone else's house, so you do need to play by their rules.

I submitted one piece to a blog as a guest post, but it wasn't what they were looking for. They came back to me with ideas for tweaks, but in the end I thought it was better to abandon the idea and do a whole new post. That one was accepted immediately and proved popular with their readers. Not being one to waste some good text (and proving that it was fine as a blog post, just not as a guest post on that particular blog) I tweaked the first one to remove references to the original blogger and published it on my own blog![39]

Once the piece has been published, have a look at it, and if there are any errors, do let the host know. Typical things to look for include spelling your name incorrectly and not putting live links on. If you spot anything like this, let them know right away and give them an opportunity to put it right. No one's perfect, and I would certainly prefer my guests to let me know if there was a problem.

Related to this, though: don't push. If you've submitted a request to guest and haven't heard back, by all means drop one reminder or question a week or so later, but that's it. For many bloggers, blogging isn't their only job. Sometimes my blog has to come second to my paid work and I'm sure other people are in that situation, too. Hassling will probably lead to a refusal!

9. Promote and share

Your guest post will build hits for and interest in both your host's blog and products / services and yours. So get promoting and sharing on their behalf, since a hit on your guest post is likely to generate a click-through to your blog or other resource. I get a lot more hits on those posts that both my guests and I promote – AND because there are more hits, the click-throughs go up, too (this is particularly noticeable on my small business chats, when it can make a big difference). So you have a vested interest in promoting the blog on which you're guesting.

---

[39] http://libroediting.com/2013/06/12/an-editor-writes-10-lessons-i-learned-when-writing-my-own-book/

One important point: don't paste the whole of your guest post into your own blog. By all means write about it and link back to the original, but duplicating content over two different blog posts will make your content disappear down the search engine rankings very fast, as the search engines are suspicious of anything that looks like automated activity and will ignore two blocks of identical text.

10. Say thank you

It's always nice to say thank you. So email the blogger who has hosted you and also put a public thank you out there on the social media. I've got a page on one of my blogs where I list my own guest post requirements but also list all the guest posts I've placed – and that sends a few people over to my hosts every day.

Social media

This section talks about social media. Why do I think that's so important for establishing a mature business? Well, I have got clients via Twitter, directly and from recommendation, and through being put in touch on Facebook. I promote my blog posts and books via Twitter, Facebook, LinkedIn and Google+. I'm a member of some interesting LinkedIn groups and chat with fellow business owners on social media, as well as my friends.

In all of this, it's important to remember that it's SOCIAL media – so it's not all about pushing out information on your latest product or sell, sell, sell. You need to put yourself into your social media usage, too, and I'm going to talk about that.

After this introduction, I'm going to run through the reasons to use social media, then focus on the main channels that I use, giving some recommendations on how best to use them. Then I'm going to talk about two very important aspects: reciprocity (i.e. politeness and, indeed, karma) in social media, and how to maintain a good online reputation. These last two are vital if you want to avoid the common pitfalls and seeing yourself, your company and your reputation going 'viral' for all of the wrong reasons!

I've put my top tips for finding freelance work via Twitter in Appendix 1, as well as information on the social media storytelling tool, Storify, in Appendix 3, as a couple of little added bonuses for you!

Read on to find out how you can have fun while raising awareness of what you do and building your customer base by optimising your use of social media.

Note: some of the instructional posts in this section are more clear if used with the accompanying screenshots. Please do pop over to the social media section of my website[40] to see these chapters expanded and with screenshots.

[40] http://libroediting.com/blog/students-small-businesses-word-users/#blog

Why use social media?

You want to grow and maintain your business, otherwise you wouldn't be reading this book. The useful thing about social media as a channel for your messages about your active and passive income generators (in my case, my services and my ebooks, but it could be your roofing repairs and affiliate links to a repair people listing site, or your personal trainer services and your downloadable fitness plans), is that you're not just talking to one person at a time; you're talking to a network.

The more you enable that network to work for you, the more news about what you do will spread. And it's free (well, almost – it costs time and there are some paid services).

How using social media helps to spread the word

When I tweet a link to a blog post, add it to my LinkedIn or Google+ profile, or update my status on Libro's Facebook page, I'm (hopefully) addressing two audiences. The first is the list of personal contacts, the ones who will see my information appear in their timelines and feeds. The second is the people to whom they could potentially carry my message.

Twitter followers, Facebook friends, LinkedIn and Google+ contact lists – what they have in common is that each is a network. Think of it like pyramid selling or chain letters but in a good way. X knows 2 people who know 2 people each, that's 4, each of those know two people and that makes 8 – even if some of them know each other, the network doubles each time.

These networks are more diverse and varied than you might at first think. Even if you're close to someone in your life, history or profession, it is unlikely that your network overlaps with theirs completely. Some examples:

- My partner of 12 years – I have 224 friends on Facebook, he has 93, but we only share 41 of those people.
- A Birmingham friend interested in the same things as me has 161 friends – and only 80 of them are shared with me.
- An old University friend, who is a freelancer like me, has just 8 friends in common out of a total of 239.
- Similarly, Libro has a certain number of individual 'likers' plus businesses.

If any of these people share my status, there's a potentially huge list of people who don't follow me personally.

It's the same on Twitter – I'm pretty sure that not all my friends' followers are following me (although it's harder to extract the figures there), so if I retweet a business's message, my followers will see their message, and if they retweet mine, theirs will know about me.

It often doesn't work directly. If I've made a good impression on someone with the information or links I share, they are more likely to remember me and, when they come across someone else in their own networks who needs something that I offer, they may well recall my details and pass my information on.

In the same way, if I tweet or put up a Facebook update about something Libro's doing, the people who see it directly from me probably know all about what I do, or they might not need a proofreader or transcriber right now. But if they share the Facebook post or retweet the tweet, who's to know who out of their wider circle might find it useful?

Much of my work comes through personal recommendation, usually from previous clients, but also through networks of friends and associates. Even large organisations need this – I was talking to someone from a museum just the other day, and he was bemoaning the lack of likes and shares on their Facebook page (which is, by the way, good, engaging and interesting). And this stuff lasts, too. A client of mine gave a friend of his my details in 2011 with regard to my transcription services for journalists. In 2013, he contacted me – via Twitter, because my details were originally shared via that channel – and became a customer.

Which social media networks should I use?

I've been keeping an eye on which social media networks work best for people doing my kind of thing (providing services) or providing physical products like craft items and cupcakes. The comments below are as a result of my personal experience and that of my friends and associates. If something we've done sounds like a good idea, by all means try it.

Facebook seems to be really good for crafty people, including jam, chutney and cupcake companies – people who MAKE something, who have a tangible to sell. People with intangible services don't seem to do quite so well – I don't get much out of my Libro Facebook page, for example, but I know 'makers' who make most of their sales through Facebook enquiries.

Twitter tends to be good for everyone. You do have to work at it, though, keeping putting your message out and – more importantly – sharing other people's messages. It's also fairly easy to seem scammy or annoy people – and nothing travels faster than a retweeted tweet, whether positive or negative.

LinkedIn is extremely useful for the corporate end of things. If you, say, provide training to corporates, or experiences, corporate gifts, that sort of thing, if you're a business advisor, health and safety consultant, anything like that, LinkedIn is the place to be (and you might even want to take out paid membership as the free membership can be a little limited).

Google+ is supposed to be growing in popularity. I have to say that I haven't got any direct work out of it, and I don't know anyone who has. However, and this is important, it does appear that sharing your content on Google+, especially if you have a company page on the site, does speed up the rate at which any content that you share gets indexed on Google itself – good news if you rely on search engine searches to find you.

Tumblr and Pinterest – I don't use these personally, but they seem to work best for people with a lot of visual content to share and talk about.

YouTube – lots of people are producing video these days, of their products or webinars and training sessions. It's vital to be on YouTube if you do any of this – and as it's owned by Google, the content, keywords and video titles make it onto that search engine that bit more quickly, too.

Do read the section above about blogging, too. A lot of what I'm talking about here relates to blogging – especially the kind of proactive blogging that involves you commenting on people's blogs and sharing posts via social media.

The most important thing to remember is to test, revisit and check what works and what doesn't. How do you do that? It's hard, but you can use these ideas to help:

- When someone contacts you to buy, ask them where they heard about you.
- If you have a website, look at your stats, especially the referrers. Where are people coming to you from? Web searches, Twitter, Facebook, other people's blogs?
- What's the reaction to the updates you post on Twitter, Facebook and LinkedIn? How many people see, like and

share, retweet or comment? Those numbers give you a good idea of your most popular channels.

Note: I would advise maintaining some sort of presence on all of the main social media channels, even if one of them seems unproductive. People do look for people and businesses on Facebook, Twitter and LinkedIn, and it's worth keeping something there for them to find. Your monitoring will, however, tell you which of them to concentrate your efforts on.

My experience

Remembering that I offer an intangible service to people, this is my experience of using social media since I started the business in 2009:

I talked about the business on Facebook from the start, before I had a Facebook page for it. I have found that friends have recommended me on to friends of theirs, and that initial contact has sometimes been via email, sometimes Facebook messages. I set up a Facebook page and get a few people 'liking' per week; Facebook has changed how it shares your page updates as it's gone down the route of charging you to advertise, so I have to share any updates on my personal feed to get a significant amount of views, likes and shares. Facebook has been good where friends, colleagues, other editors and editors' organisations and other small businesses have shared my updates – this can push powerful numbers of viewers over to my blog to find out more.

I used Twitter to search for clients in the early days, and you can read more about how to do that in Appendix 1. Nowadays I use it more for sharing my blog posts and other people's content. I get a fair number of retweets, where people share my comments and content, and like interacting with my clients on there. I can't overestimate how powerful it was for getting me long-term, paying clients and, if I was looking to build my roster of customers again, I would certainly go there first.

Google+ is something I auto-post to, I get the odd +1 (its version of a like) but it doesn't do that much for me – except for the fact that my posts shared there hit the search engine index faster.

LinkedIn groups are useful for interacting with other people in business or the same industry. I do find that the groups get full of people just posting out their content without sharing or commenting on other people's, so do have a careful look at any group you want to join to check the signal to noise ratio.

Now let's look at the major social media channels that you can use in a little more detail (note that these are correct at the time of publication; the channels do have a habit of changing how things are done).

Using Facebook for your business

You can set up a page for your business on Facebook as long as you've got a personal login.

The slight issue with Facebook business pages is that Facebook wants you to pay for adverts and to have your posts and page promoted to other people. So do be prepared to receive lots of suggestions to pay for ads and promotion, and not a lot of interaction from other users.

How to set up a Facebook business page

You will need to be logged in to Facebook:

Go to www.facebook/pages/create and choose a category of page to create.

If, for example, you choose company / organisation, you then need to choose your category and give your page a name. If you choose local business or place, you're given space to enter your address – good if you have a shop, not really recommended if you operate from your home and don't want all and sundry to know your address.

Whatever type of page you set up, you will be asked to tick that you accept Facebook's Page terms and conditions.[41] These include a host of stipulations about promotions, advertising, tagging and other issues. Note that Facebook can remove admin rights and shut down your page if you don't abide by these rules. This is why I would never suggest limiting your web presence to only a Facebook page – make sure that you have your own website, too.

---

[41] https://www.facebook.com/page_guidelines.php

Once you've set up your page, you can set up a cover for your page and a profile picture. You can upload these from your current Facebook albums or your computer's drives. There are all sorts of rules about what you can have here, but they change frequently, so refer to the current terms and conditions. You can change these pictures by hovering over them, at which point a button will appear offering you the opportunity to do so.

When you've created your basic page, you can add information and details as you wish. Use the Update Page Info button to access these options:

Page info allows you to describe your business and add hours of operation, etc. You don't have to fill in everything, but it is useful to add your website's URL, for example. You can change this information at any time.

Settings allows you to set out who can post on the page and other features. This is useful if you have people putting spam comments, etc., on the page – you can set it so that only you can post. However, I do like to let people post and comment to foster a sense of community. It's worth looking at this area frequently, as what you can and can't do does change over time.

Admin roles allows you to add other people who can administrate the page – useful if you've set up the page but you have someone in your company who's a social media expert. It's also useful to have someone else with an admin role if you get locked out of Facebook, or are incapacitated for any reason.

You'll also see a **view page** button at the top of the screen which allows you to return to the page at any time.

Once your page is all set up, you will see an Admin panel at the top, above your page cover picture (it might be just a line of buttons, in which case hit the Show button on the right to see the full panel).

This lets you know how often your posts have been seen and the viewing figures. Note that these are likely to be distressingly small – see the section on paying for promotion below.

Interacting with people on your page

You can post updates on your page, including photos and notes, just like you can on your personal Facebook timeline. I send my blog post notifications to this page – but then I share them to my personal timeline, too, where they have more chance of being seen.

When you Like a page belonging to someone else, you can click on the down-arrow by Message and Like as your page – this will appear in their timeline and can lead to some nice, friendly interaction.

If you have set your page up to accept comments by others, do pop by the page to respond to these – a) it's polite to reply to comments and b) you need to watch out for spam and complaints, and address them accordingly.

Stopping spam and dealing with complaints

It is possible to delete comments that other people make on your Facebook page. Just be aware that if you delete complaints, the complainer is liable to share the fact that you've done that – a bit of polite damage limitation on the page itself is often more appropriate.

If someone spams my page, for example they've just posted a link to their page, I usually reply politely the first time (especially if it's vaguely relevant) in case they've made a mistake, otherwise they get deleted.

If you're considering paying for promotion on Facebook ...

Whenever I get tempted to advertise on Facebook (and they do promise to target your selected audience), I think about the random /

odd / offensive / inappropriate adverts that I see on my timeline, and that makes me think that it's perhaps not worth it.

If you do decide to pay for advertising, go for one of the pay per click options where you can limit how much you pay out per day. Observe how it goes very carefully, and try to assess how much business you're actually getting for what you pay for (see the section on Investing in Your Business).

The golden rule of Facebook business pages

There's a golden rule that applies to all social media and that's Be Yourself. Allow your own personal self to appear on those pages. Have a picture of you on the profile, and comment and respond as appropriate.

It's also worth noting that your friends do not want to feel spammed by your business. I share my business page posts once at most onto my personal timeline. I don't leap in to every personal conversation with "Oh, I can proofread that" or "need some transcription, just call me". It isn't appropriate, none of us like having that done to us, and it's a good way to annoy those very people who might otherwise be spreading the word about your business. By all means, mix business with pleasure, but make your business page pleasurable to read and keep your personal page personal as well as businesslike.

When considering this, also consider that if there's an obvious link between your business and personal pages, either keep the personal pages locked down to Friends only or be careful to represent yourself more professionally than you might if you used Facebook purely in a personal capacity.

Using Twitter for your business

Twitter is an absolutely brilliant tool for business owners – if you use it in the right way. If you use in the wrong way, it can be a nightmare, as bad (or embarrassing) news travels very fast in the Twitterverse!

I personally got a lot out of Twitter in the early days, the long-term clients I secured using it recommended me on to others, too. I'd go as far as to say that it's my number four source of work, after repeat business, personal recommendations and the Proz website. Benefits of Twitter: it's quick and easy to use. Disadvantage: it can be a time-sink. Most important thing to remember: People only tend to see a snapshot of their tweets every day. I only know one person who reads ALL of the tweets in his timeline. This means that your tweeting strategy should be a bit different from your other social media posting strategies.

Setting up your Twitter profile

When you join Twitter, it's very quick and easy to set up your profile, which is a quick guide to who you are. Anyone clicking on it or searching for it needs to know that they've found the right Liz Broomfield / Libro (or whatever) and to see easily what you do.

I would recommend including the following on your profile, and I've seen plenty of other people recommend this, too:

- Your real name when you log in, as well as your company name for your Twitter ID
- Your photograph on your profile, rather than your company logo (you can add that to your background)
- Your company URL in the field where you can provide that
- Use your 140 letters of profile to the max, including what you do and any extra URLs (shortened using a service such as bit.ly[42])

As with any profile, you can change it at any point; just click on the cog icon Settings and Help and choose Edit profile. (For more on how to edit your profile see Appendix 1.)

Following and followers

Once you've set up your Twitter account, you can start following a few people. Twitter will suggest ones that you don't really want, based on who's popular, but you can find interesting people to follow in a variety of ways:

- Ask someone for their Twitter ID when you meet them, or glean it from their business card or website. Then enter that ID in the search field on Twitter or go to www.twitter.com/[ID without the @ sign] and press the Follow button.
- Search for the person's name or company name in the search field on Twitter. Have a look at their profile to check it's the correct person, and press the Follow button.
- If you're following someone in an interesting field, have a look at who they're following. If you click on their profile, you will see links to Tweets, Following and Followers. Click on Following and have a look – there will be a handy Follow button by each name so you can simply follow from there.

Once you're viewing who someone is following, you will see a menu to the left which includes an entry for Lists. See more about Lists later on, but you can follow either an entire list or members of one by clicking on the list, and this is another good way to glean people to follow in a particular area of interest.

How do I choose who to follow?

---

[42] http://www.bit.ly/

It's entirely up to you how many people you follow and whether you organise them in any way. When I'm deciding whether to follow people who I've found, or who have followed me (you don't HAVE to follow everyone who's followed you, but it's polite to have a look at least), this is what I do:

- Check their profile to see whether they're interesting to me
- Check their list of tweets to see if they tweet interesting information
- Check that they're legitimate, that they are representing the company they say they are or, if famous in your field or generally, they are who they say they are
- Check their tweets for the same tweet repeated over and over again – this means a lack of imagination, something akin to spamming or an automated response
- Check their tweets for regularity and date of tweeting – if someone tweets once a week or hasn't tweeted for a number of months, unless they're hugely important to me, I won't bother to follow them because their tweets will get lost in the general melee

I do also regularly run a check over the people I'm following (click on the Me link at the top of the screen and follow the menu down to Following) to make sure they're still active. If not, I tend to cull. Sorry!

Lists

Lists are a great way to put the people who you follow into categories or filters that you can look at independently. For example, I have a "Must know" list which includes all of the real-life friends plus some news feeds that I follow, so that if I only have time for a quick dip into Twitter, I can see what's really important. I also have a "Journos" one so that I can see what my music journalist clients and a few others are up to, for some entertainment.

To add someone to a list:

- Go to your list of accounts followed (Me – Following)
- Click the User Options button (next to Following, it looks like a head with a down arrow next to it)
- Click on Add or Remove From Lists
- You'll see a list of all of the lists you've already set up (if you have set any up) plus a button, Create a List
- Either click on a list name to add that person or Create a List and make up a new list name to add this person to
- Note: you can add people who you're not actually following to Lists, meaning that they don't clog up your Twitter feed but you can still keep up to date

Once you have some lists, you'll see a Lists entry on the left hand side when you click on Me. Ideas for lists include friends, particular interests, your business sector, news feeds, sport – anything you want.

You can follow other people's lists or mine them for good accounts to follow – just click on a particular person's Twitter ID and you'll get their following, followers and lists.

Note – this doesn't work exactly the same on mobile devices or third-party Twitter management dashboards as it does on the basic web-based Twitter interface. These instructions are for the latter.

How Twitter works - @ and #

You'll see a lot of the symbols @ and # on Twitter.

@ is used in front of a Twitter ID to notify the person that you're talking to them or to point someone else to their account. For example, someone might recommend an account for me to follow:

MD: @lyzzybee_libro have a look at @thecreativepenn for a good feed for writers

This makes the message appear in my Connect list (see below) and TheCreativePenn's Connect list, so I will see the recommendation and she will see that she's been recommended to me. If she wants, she can then reach out to me, and say thank you to MD.

is used to create clickable links that will pull information on a particular topic together in one view. It's often used at events and conferences – so, for example, #cbsms is used by people tweeting about the Central Birmingham Social Media Surgery. When you see a hashtag (as this is called) in a tweet, it will be a clickable link. Click on the hashtag and you will see all of the recent tweets with that hashtag, giving you a view of what's going on and who's talking about it.

Lyzzbee_libro: Off to the social media surgery to help a few people today #cbsms

It is also used to link tweets on a wider topic, e.g. #amwriting, which writers use to talk about the writing process. You can pop a hashtag on a tweet when you want it to come up in such searches, for example I might tweet about my book on transcription and add #transcription at the end, so that anyone looking at that hashtag will see my tweet.

Your Twitterstream and mentions

Whether you're viewing Twitter online on a computer or via a phone or a third party dashboard, you will have a twitterstream and then various other views.

Your twitterstream will show you all the most recent tweets by people / companies / whatever that you're following.

Your Connect list will show you anything directly concerning your own Twitter account – so messages that have been sent to you with an @[your Twitter ID] as well as people who have followed you. It's good practice to keep an eye on this so that you can reply to any messages sent to you and say thank you for recommendations and follows.

Getting rid of spammers

Everyone gets spammed by Twitter accounts, dodgy or otherwise, that are usually either looking for random followers to boost their numbers or clicks to their undesirable links. The ones with links often only have a link in the text – this is a real red flag and you should never click on a link in a tweet, even from a friend, if there's only a link and no text (your friend could have had their account hacked).

If you receive an odd tweet or one with just a link, click on the photo or name of the sender. You will typically see that they've sent the same short message or no message and link to multiple people. Click on the User Actions button on their profile and you have options to Block @[Twitter ID] or Report @[Twitter ID] for spam. If you do the latter, it will block them anyway. It's best to do this as it alerts Twitter that the person is spamming, and will help to save someone not as savvy as you from clicking on a dodgy link and going who knows where in cyberspace!

If you're just getting annoyed or bored by a Twitter account that you follow, you can click on their photo or name and press the button marked Following – this will change to Unfollow as you hover over it; click it and you'll unfollow them and no longer see them in your Twitterstream.

Rules for using Twitter effectively

Using Twitter effectively is a matter of knowing how it works and how people view it, and being sensible and polite.

1. Posting multiple times

The main point about tweeting is that very few people read every single tweet on their timeline. People typically check Twitter on the way to work, at lunchtime, on the way home, and some time in the evening. Once you're following more than about fifty people, there's no way that you're going to see all of their tweets – so think of people as viewing a snapshot of their Twitterstream rather than everything.

This means that it's fine to tweet a message multiple times, where it would be seen as rude and intrusive to post a Facebook status multiple times in one day (if you connect your Twitter to your Facebook, set up some means of selectively posting to Facebook only once, rather than automating all tweets over there. You can use #fb to autopost to Facebook once you have the link set up).

You also need to be aware of your markets and their time zones – if you have a lot of Australian clients, and you're in the UK, you will need to tailor your tweets to their time zone, maybe investing in a Twitter dashboard that will allow you to pre-schedule your tweets.

2. Using a dashboard

It can be very useful to use a dashboard such as Hootsuite or Tweetdeck to manage your Twitter accounts. You can view multiple accounts at a time and post as them (handy if you have, say, a personal and a work account) and view your lists in their own feeds. Some of them will also allow you to schedule your tweets to be published at a certain time or on a certain date, which can be very useful (although watch out that you still keep an eye on when these go out, as there have been numerous examples of an auto-tweet posting when it's really not appropriate, such as after a disaster).

3. Sharing other people's material

The other main rule is to be polite and reciprocate and say thank you.

If you retweet other people's tweets, they are more likely to share your tweets with their network. To retweet, click on the word retweet underneath the tweet, or look for that 'arrows-in-a-square' icon which has the same effect. To modified retweet (retweet with a comment / MT), copy and paste the person's tweet with a comment of your own or select the option on some mobile apps or dashboards. Some people reckon that you should share five other tweets to every one of your own that you post. I'm not that scientific, but I do try to share as much as I post.

4. Saying thank you and being proactive

If other people retweet or otherwise share your tweets, which you will find out about by reviewing your Connect feed, do drop them a message to say thank you.

If someone recommends your Twitter account or your services to someone else, contact the person to whom you're being recommended with a polite "how can I help you?" and a way to contact you. Don't forget to say thank you to the recommender.

5. Not automating too much and not spamming

I'm not a big fan of automated messages when I follow someone's Twitter account, and I know many other people find them annoying, too. I like to know that there's a person behind the account. Similarly, all sales and no sharing, or all automated tweeting and no replying to @ messages will probably get people irritated.

Using LinkedIn for your business

LinkedIn is seen primarily as a networking tool for the more corporate end of the market. However, you can set up your own business page on LinkedIn now, and there is a lot more interactivity and 'social' activity than there used to be – or than you might think.

Setting up a LinkedIn profile

Once on www.linkedin.com, you can join up and set up your profile. It's a good idea to include as much information as you can on here – and in a professional way. It's never a good idea to allow typos and grammatical errors on any professional profile, and it's vitally important here, as people tend to make more of an effort, so any errors will be very glaring.

There are various sections to fill in on the profile; including past jobs allows your 'network' to grow, as LinkedIn, unlike other social media, will not let you even request to connect to just anyone.

Finding your way around LinkedIn

Your home page will contain a feed a little like your Facebook timeline, with updates from people to whom you're linked. To find people to link to, you can search in the search box at the top of the screen. Once you're linked to someone, they will appear in your Connections list, which you can access by clicking the [number] connections icon to the bottom right of your profile picture area.

Your profile also includes a link to People You May Know. This will give you people in networks connected to you by other connections, workplaces or interest groups to whom you might want to link.

You can see your invitations and notifications at the top right:

- Invitations allow you to see who has invited you to connect and any messages they've sent you via LinkedIn
- Notifications show you who has liked your updates or shared your profile

Linking to people on LinkedIn

LinkedIn is different from other social media networks, in that you have to have a tangible connection to a person in order to 'Link' to them. If you find someone you want to link to and press Connect, you'll be asked how you know that person. If you say that they're a colleague, or that you've done business with them, you'll be asked which of your jobs they are a colleague from – that's why it's important to list all of the companies that you have worked for on your profile. If you say that they're a friend, you'll be asked to prove you know them by providing their email address.

You can find people just outside your network by clicking on the People You May Know link. This will give you a list of either friends of friends or people who have said that they work or have worked at the same organisations that you've worked at. You can connect to these people in the same way.

Setting up a company page

You can set up a company page on LinkedIn for your business – this will give people another way to find you and will provide another link to your website and other social media.

To set up a company page, click on Interests at the top, then Companies from the drop-down. At the top right of the next page you'll find a link for Add Company. You will first need to confirm that you're eligible to create and moderate this page, so there will be an email sent to you to confirm, and you must have a personal LinkedIn account to create a company page. Fill in all of your company's details and save – and there you go.

To edit your company information, go and find the company page and click on Edit.

Getting social

This section is about social media – so how do you get social on LinkedIn?

- Updates

You can post updates, just like on Facebook – do this from the Home page. Your updates will appear on your connections' home pages, just as theirs do on yours. You can like and share updates in a very similar way to Facebook.

You can direct most blogging platforms to automatically post links on LinkedIn – all of my WordPress blog posts do this. You can also link your Twitter account to LinkedIn by going to your account settings (click on the small photo in the top right of the screen), clicking on your name and choosing Manage Twitter Accounts.

- Recommendations and endorsements

If someone has done a good job for you, you can click on Recommend in their profile and type in a recommendation. They will be emailed this and will have the option as to whether to publish it or not (this prevents people posting negative comments without the member knowing). Endorsements allow you to click on a button to confirm that the person in question has a particular skill – this can be very useful when you're looking at profiles but be aware that anyone can add any skill to your profile, and this might not match what you actually do – you will be alerted by email if someone does this and can delete the odd skill.

- Groups

There are thousands of interest groups on LinkedIn and these can be a good way to meet new people, spread the word about what you're doing, and find out what other people are up to.

Access Groups by searching in the top search bar (you can click on the icon to the left of the search area and select only Groups to search) or by clicking on Interests then Groups. Once you've joined some Groups, you will find them listed on your Groups page, and then some suggestions underneath.

Groups work very simply – you can post a new message or reply to another one, just like in other social media like Facebook and Google+. You can choose whether you are updated by email for all posts and replies in the group, or whether you want to just access them via the LinkedIn website.

I have found that some groups do become clogged with too many adverts and not enough discussion, but others can be really useful. The usual rules apply about reciprocity and kindness when using LinkedIn for social media communications.

Golden rules for using LinkedIn

- Be professional. LinkedIn is known as a professional and careers-orientated site, although there is certainly room for the self-employed. But you do need to be extra professional and not very personal on here.
- Reciprocate – if people like and share your updates and group posts, say thank you and like and share theirs.
- Similarly, if people recommend or endorse you, do try to recommend and endorse them back.

Using Google+ for your business

Google+ is a relatively new entrant to the social media arena, and people still seem to be a bit confused about its value and use.

The most important feature of Google+ is that content mentioned on the platform will be indexed by the Google search engine that bit quicker.

So it's worth signing up for a Google account (I recommend using Gmail for your email anyway, as it has a large capacity and you can attach your own email address to it and forward other emails to it), using Google+ and even setting up a company page.

Setting up a Google+ account

Once you have a Google account, you automatically have a Google+ account. If you're viewing your Gmail account, you will see a square of nine smaller squares in the top menu bar to the right (this does change regularly, so look for anything marked Apps). Click and you'll have the option to access Google+ or G+. You can also access it via the url https://plus.google.com/

Your profile

When you first click into Google+, you will be asked to create your public profile by adding a photo, etc. You can update your profile at any time. Your Google picture will appear in the top right, or an icon if you don't have a picture – click on the icon and you can view your profile. You can then add a picture, a background and updates, much like with Facebook.

Your connections

Your connections are called your Circles, and the unique selling point here is that you add people to Circles, or lists of kinds of people, right from the start – so you can differentiate between friends, family and colleagues and then share information to different groups very easily.

If someone adds you to their Circles, you have the option to add them back, which is just like Friending on Facebook.

Business pages

As you share information and links from your blog and website to your Google+, they will be quickly indexed by Google. Add your business and its website address and this will be further promoted.

Click on the home button and down to Pages. Click on Pages. You'll reach a pages home page and find a link Create a Page. Choose the type of business, business sector, then add all of your company details, including your company's website address. You will be prompted to connect your page to Google+ and you will be emailed a link to this Google+ page which you can paste onto your own website's home page. Once you've done that, you're a verified Google+ business.

Golden rules of Google+

The rules here are the same as everywhere:

- Be professional
- Reciprocate and share

Reciprocity in social media

Here's a guide to how to be polite on social media, so as to 'leverage your social capital' (which actually just means make social media work for you) and use sharing and friendliness to help yourself and others.

It's all about **reciprocity**. What does that mean?

What is reciprocity?

The dictionary definition of reciprocity is gaining mutual benefit from exchanging things with other people.

In the case of social media (in which I include blogging), done well it should be a two-way and mutual activity, this means building strands of connection which can, over time, turn into powerful networks that can help you start, grow or develop your business or other endeavour.

By responding to comments and forging links, sharing and re-tweeting, you make yourself more prominent in other people's eyes, *for the right reasons.*

If you are unfailingly polite, share people's content, always say thank you, share people's details with other people and act as an ambassador and connector for other people's personal brands as well as your own, that will come back to you in bucketfuls.

Whether you're just starting out, embracing a new form of social media, or need a gentle reminder (I know that writing this reminded me to return to sharing more on Twitter), I hope you find these tips useful.

Reciprocity on Twitter

Use Twitter to forge links, have short conversations, support and encourage others and share content with your followers. People who you retweet will be more likely to retweet your posts. People who you recommend to others will remember the favour. So:

- Always respond to @ comments that require a reply (i.e. they ask you a question or tell you about something).
- Always respond to RTs, Follow Friday ('ff') mentions, etc., with a thank you Tweet.
- If someone recommends you to someone else, always a) thank the original person, b) make contact with the prospect – don't wait for them to come to you.
- Take part in peer-group events like #watercoolermoment etc. to encourage the people who run them and engage with your peers – you are likely to find new, interesting people to follow and talk to.
- Retweet other people's content if it's interesting to you / your followers. People often talk about the 80/20 rule – eight retweets or shares of other people's content via the social media sharing buttons on their blog posts to every two promoting your own words or interests.

Note: Twitter works fast. Many people don't see their whole stream, just snapshots through the day. If someone has seen your content and contacted you / shared, etc., try to thank them within 12 hours or less.

Not sure what I'm on about with all this talk of @ and RTs and followers and # signs? Have a look at the "Using Twitter for your business" chapter above.

Reciprocity on Facebook

This applies mainly to people using Facebook for their business, however it helps keep the wheels of general social interaction running smoothly, too!

- If someone asks a question on your business page or a business-related question on your own timeline, always respond. My business page doesn't always alert me when I have a new comment – so keep checking yours to make sure you're not ignoring someone!
- If someone sends you a Facebook message, always respond if it's appropriate and meant for you, not spam.
- Check your 'other' messages for messages from people who are not 'friends' with you but are making genuine contact, and respond appropriately.
- If people comment on your status updates, 'like' their comments and engage with them.
- If people share your status updates, 'like' the share and say thank you publicly or privately.
- If people recommend you via Facebook, thank the recommender and contact the prospect as soon as you can.
- Share other people's content.
- Like business pages as yourself and as your business (click on the cog next to the message).
- If you join groups of peers, people in the same business, people who are also self-employed, etc., join in with the group once you're there, help other people and don't either relentlessly self-promote or stay silent.

Facebook works on friendship and commonality. Share your peers' posts and you'll build up a network of people who will recommend, help and support you.

Reciprocity on blogs

I'm including blogs in social media because the best blogs that work well for businesses and people who want a 'successful' blog are those that engage in two-way conversation, share content and link people together. Sounds like social media to me! I've said a lot about this in the chapter on blogging, above, but here's a reminder of a few key points:

- On your own blog, mention and link to people who have helped, advised or inspired you.
- ALWAYS reply to comments. If you don't have time to reply to each individually, at least put up a thank you and a mention to the most important ones.
- Keep an eye on your search statistics and respond to what your readers are looking for (e.g. I noticed people were searching for "comment boxes too large" so added a new blog post about that).
- If people like and comment on your blog, pop over to their blog and scatter a few comments and likes if you find their content interesting.
- Use those social media buttons on other people's blogs to share their content – and make sure you enable the ones on your blog to allow and encourage people to share.
- Engage with other bloggers especially in your industry sector or area of interest – comment, share, etc.
- Offer guest post spots on your blog for other people to contribute content.
- If you give someone a guest blog spot, make sure that you include all their links as well as a little biography about them. Make it easy for people to find them.
- If you place a guest post on someone else's blog, make sure that you give them all of your links to include, and talk about it as much as possible on your other social media channels.

Blogs can be a powerful way to meet people, link with people, learn from people and get your content shared around the world.

Reciprocity on LinkedIn

LinkedIn can be a very powerful tool for IT and other business people, with most recruiters looking for a LinkedIn profile these days. Make sure that your full CV is on there, and a good photo. Here's how to keep things professional and reciprocal on LinkedIn:

- When you link to someone, change the standard message to a personal one, maybe reminding them where you met or making another tailored comment. Some people get quite annoyed with the standard messages and might even ignore then on principle, so it's worth making that extra effort.
- Introduce people who you think would be useful to each other.
- Press that endorse button and give your contact some more stats.
- Use the recommend feature if you've worked with someone to place some feedback on their profile, LinkedIn displays how many recommendations you've made, and everyone wants to work with someone who's generous with feedback and honest praise.
- If someone endorses or recommends you, or introduces you to a third party, send them a message to say thank you.
- Join groups and share content kindly and generously.
- When you join a group, get to know people and comment on other posts and questions before you start self-promoting.
- If a group seems to be full of spam and self-promotion and no discussion and mutual encouragement, leave it alone – you won't be able to change it and it'll just annoy you. But learn what not to do from that!

Reciprocity on Google+

Google+ works much like Facebook, in that you can +1 posts, make comments etc. The major point about Google+ is that if you share your content and others' on there, Google will pick up on it that little bit quicker to add it to its search engine. So it's worth engaging on there even if it isn't as busy or active as the other networks (or maybe it is in your field?).

Reciprocity on Pinterest, Tumblr, etc.

I've talked here about the social media networks that I use. I don't know much about Pinterest, Tumblr, etc., so I'm not going to go into detail, but the same basics apply: share people's posts, thank them for their interest, make it a share-share-share thing rather than a me-me-me thing.

How to maintain a good online reputation

You are your brand. I know that that sounds a bit marketing-speaky, but it's true. If you run a business, people are going to look for you online as well as your business name. I can vouch for that, because I get loads of searches coming through to my blog for the people I feature in my Small Business Chat. Far more of them are looking for the person's name than for their business name (if it's different). In this chapter, I'm going to talk about my personal methods for maintaining a good and positive online image, with some tips which should be useful for you, too.

These tips mostly relate to social media, but you can extend them to anywhere where people see you, and your business, in operation, such as networking events, trade fairs, etc.

What do you mean by "You are your brand"?

This is particularly important if you run a small business or are a sole trader. However, even if you look at a multinational, the person at the head of the company and the reputation they personally have has an effect on the perception of the company.

Think about Richard Branson. What about Theo Paphitis and Duncan Bannatyne? Remember Gerald Ratner and how he ruined his business with one sentence?[43]

In the same way, when you go out networking, or you do stuff online, and you run a business (or even if you don't), people are getting an impression of you which extends to the perception they have of your business.

---

[43] http://en.wikipedia.org/wiki/Gerald_Ratner

My personal dos and don'ts

This is of course a personal list. Maybe you disagree? I know that I'm ultra-careful about my brand and company reputation, but I'd rather be ultra-careful than too relaxed. Reputations can be destroyed in an instant!

This is not about manipulating your image to sell more of your product or service; it's about making sure that you're representing your company in a positive light and making sure you match in your behaviour the message that you want your business to get across.

- DO be yourself

It's no good trying to hide who you are. Yes, if you're shy, you can project more of an image of self-assurance, but also kindness, respect and care often come with shyness, and they're good things for your clients to see. Personally, I'm very open and honest, and I try to give something back through charity donations and helping people. Therefore I have made small business loans to celebrate Libro's anniversary[44] and help out other small businesses with my weekly features,[45] etc. I also keep my blog posts linked to what I do and my own practices – someone mentioned to me just the other day that my posts are very personal and friendly – which is how I hope my business comes across, too.

- DO stay true to your morals and ideals

As an addition to this, I try to make sure that what I do with Libro mirrors my own personal morals and ideals. This is why I won't put ads on my blogs (unless it's a testimonial for someone whose work I know is good), and why I am very careful about the guest blog posts I publish. I recently turned down a fair amount of money offered to

---

[44] http://libroediting.com/2012/08/01/happy-birthday-libro/
[45] http://libroediting.com/blog/all-the-interviews/

me to mention a blog-hosting company on a blog post, because I was asked not to disclose that it was a sponsored post. Not my thing. I have also turned down work because of my personal ideals.

- DO be human

If you have a personal presence on social media, and even if you only have a business presence, make sure that the person behind the business shows through. This applies especially if you're sharing your business posts on your personal account. I have a Libro Facebook page[46] (where I make sure you can see photos of me and ask for feedback as well as sharing my blog posts) and a personal Facebook page, and I try to make sure I post more personal than business stuff on the personal page. People want to know the person behind the business, and they particularly don't want the friend they've followed to turn into a corporate mouthpiece all of a sudden.

- DON'T bombard friends with your business message

It's very tempting to repost all of your business blog postings, etc. on to your personal Facebook and Twitter streams. It's even more tempting to shoehorn a mention of your business into every comment you make to your friends. We all know at least one person who does this (I've been accused of it myself by one person, but I do try hard to keep the balance), and what does it do? It puts you off buying their goods or service. Sorry, but it does. Do share your business stuff with your friends, but not at the expense of the normal friend stuff!

- DON'T moan about your customers

This one is oh-so-tempting, too. Especially if you work alone, sometimes you have to MOAN. Here's the thing: moan, but don't do

---

[46] http://www.facebook.com/Libroediting

it in public. Really, don't. If you only follow one of these tips, follow this one. If you moan about a customer, even 'just' on your personal Facebook timeline, how many of your friends might have been going to recommend your services to a friend, and might now not be inclined to. It's unprofessional.

Of course, we do all need to moan, but this is what you do: do it in private. I set up a local homeworkers' support group and an "Editors' Rah and Argh" group on Facebook – as private, invitation-only groups. If we want to roar, sob or moan, we do it there, or in an email to a friend, or in a cafe, not in public!

- DON'T talk about your customers at all, actually

Not only the moaning, but be careful what you say about your clients in public. I have Non-Disclosure Agreements with some of mine, which means no talking, ever, but even with the others, I do not identify them by name, when talking in public or writing about them in my book. I don't Tweet to my music journalist clients, outing myself as their transcriber, unless they specifically mention it in public first. I don't put their comments on my references page and CV before asking first. It's just good practice.

- DON'T let people see the frantic paddling, just the serene swan

Cash flow problems or upset by something? I might mention in the most general terms that I'm feeling a bit stressed, but I usually won't. Although it's good to talk things out, if you run a business, you don't know who is watching. If you would be worried if a customer or prospect saw what you were writing, do it privately – create a filter or a private group on Facebook. If in doubt, don't talk about it in public.

- DO be appropriate

If you manage rock bands and hang out at heavy metal festivals, by all means swear a bit on your public tweets. If you earn your living editing, try not to have spelling mistakes and typos all over your blog (this is really hard to do – I know. Collect a group of friendly people who will let you know privately if such a thing occurs). I lead a pretty quiet life, but I do try not to swear or have inappropriate pictures of me all over social media. Obviously that's easier the older you are and the less of your adult life has been lived in the full glare of social media, but you can always politely ask people to untag you from that hen party pic or horrendous shot from your younger days. If you explain politely that your business is linked to your name, and you're worried about affecting it, most people will surely comply with that! You can also untag yourself from Facebook posts and pictures and set up your profile so that you have to approve all tags, if you're at all worried .

My golden rule for maintaining a good online reputation

This is my golden rule. I've stuck by it ever since I started having an online presence:

Never say anything in public online that you wouldn't be happy shouting out loud in the middle of Birmingham (or Leeds, or London, or your nearest big city).

Afterword: Where do you go next?

So, you've got through the start-up phase, you've got a decent business going, and you're still getting enquiries from prospective new customers. You might be earning enough to be thinking about optimising your tax situation or even going VAT-registered. What do you do now?

You have various options: in this section I'm going to run through the main ones, and I recommend popping over to my website to read the additional material I'm building up there: expert advice from solicitors and accountants, business consultants and the like, who will talk us through the options, AND real-life examples from people who've been there and done it and can share their experiences.[47]

In summary, here's what you can do:

- Go full time if you're not already
- Outsource tasks to other companies
- Turn yourself into a Limited Company
- Get VAT-registered
- Employ people
- Contract out to other freelancers
- Go into partnership with someone
- Expand into premises – an office or workshop
- Do nothing

Going full time with your business

If you're not already full time, and you're feeling pressured by having a day job and your own business, it can be very worthwhile going it alone. I've written a whole book on the subject,[48] but I know

---

[47] http://libroediting.com/2013/11/25/developing-your-business/
[48] http://librofulltime.wordpress.com/e-book-going-it-alone-at-40/

lots of people who've done this: it can be hard to decide when to jump ship, but very rewarding when you do!

Outsourcing

Outsourcing means getting someone else to do tasks such as:

- Admin
- Finance
- HR
- Sales
- Telemarketing

Outsourcing the admin and sales effort allows you to devote your time to working at the actual tasks that form the core of your work. More billable hours should mean more money coming in, and you can accommodate more clients. You can find articles on the Libro blog about tasks that you can outsource and I covered how to work out whether it's worth it in the section on "Investing in your business", above.

Becoming a Limited Company or going VAT registered

Both of these options have reputation and tax implications. Some clients in some industries find that dealing with a Limited Company or someone with a VAT number represents solidity and safety (of course, sometimes, it can be a disadvantage, for example, if you are VAT registered yourself but most of your clients aren't, they won't be able to claim back the VAT that they pay to you). Becoming a Limited Company can protect you legally, which is essential in some sectors and save you some tax (legally and ethically). Always take advice on whether you need to be Limited, have particular insurances, etc.

Employing people, contracting out work or going into partnership

These all involve getting other people into your business to share the workload. Some companies will contract out to people who do the same thing. For example, I work for a company that deals in proofreading for students: they send the work to me and pay me when I invoice them, and they invoice the customer for a bit more. If you go down this route, it involves a lot of admin on both sides, but it means that you can have multiple people working for you without going down the employing them route. It brings in profit on their work without doing that work yourself (there are laws about when someone's an employee, though, so it can get tricky). You can read more about employing people on my blog.

Going into a partnership involves a legal setup but can be useful if you have complementary skills. You have to think carefully about who you do this with, though, and issues like where you'll work and who is responsible for what.

Employing people involves a lot of legal stuff and means that you're responsible for other people's income and taxes, but there are freelance HR companies out there that can help.

You could also investigate offering franchises in your business or taking on an apprentice. Franchising has a lot of rules and regulations but allows you to replicate your brand and success with managers in place to run the businesses, and apprentices are given external training as well as working with you.

Moving into business premises

If it feels like you've outgrown your home office and you want more room for making the goods you sell, or you want to separate home and work life a bit better, then moving into premises can be the next step. This does involve costs, although there are offers out there that give you secretarial and reception support which can be very useful. It can look more professional if people visit you, too. Beware the treadmill that leads to getting more office space / employing more people / getting more space / employing more people, with your overheads going up and up, unless you have a steady head and a good accountant! But it does work very well for some people.

Doing nothing

I have to admit that this is my approach. Why? Mainly because what I do is so linked to me, my style of editing, my relationship with my clients, and because I like being my own boss, beholden to no one and responsible for no one. Most editors work like this, but I have looked at what some peers in other businesses have done, and realised I'd rather keep my simple model). However, as you'll know if you have read this book all the way from the beginning, I have done this:

- Contracted out my accounting to allow me to devote my time to work, not admin
- Developed robust business routines for the same reason
- Optimised my customer base to give me a good mix of work and a good income stream
- Worked on developing passive income streams
- Developed a network of people to whom I can refer new business or the occasional bit of overflow work from regular customers

This is where I am now: happily running a mature business, nice and busy, with a fairly predictable cash flow, clients in different sectors, countries and areas of work to balance each other out, and with a home and personal life as well as a work life. I hope that this book will help you to reach the same point – or wherever you're aiming to be.

Read on for some appendices about very specific tools and practices, after which you can find out a little bit more about me and my other books. Thanks for reading this far!

Appendix 1: How to search for a job on Twitter

I had planned to write about exactly how I would go about searching for jobs on Twitter, then ended up discussing the topic with another editor, who's keen on working on cookery books. So, here comes a worked example of how to search for jobs on Twitter. Note: pop over to my blog[49] for all of the screen shots and additional resources.

Why search for jobs on Twitter?

People talk a LOT on Twitter, and they also use it for information seeking purposes. How many times have you seen someone you follow ask a question, or look for a recommendation? People will throw a question out: "Does anyone know a good transcriber?" and other people will answer them. It's brilliant if one of your own clients answers a request like this and gives your name (this happens quite regularly to me, so I promise it happens), but if not, as long as you're not over-pushy about it, there is no harm in tweeting to that person to tell them about your services.

Does searching for jobs on Twitter really work?

Yes. Yes it does. I can say that with certainty, because I know from experience. Here are just a couple of examples:

1. I ran my regular search (see below for how to do this) on "looking for proofreader". I found a Tweet by a woman working in PR. I contacted her, she became a client, she took me with her when she joined a big agency, and when she left that agency, I ended up with them as well as her as clients.

---

[49] http://libroediting.com/2013/12/23/searching-for-jobs-on-twitter/

2. A journalist I followed on Twitter posted the tweet "Can anyone help me with some transcription?" At the time, I didn't offer transcription as a service, but I was a trained audio-typist. I got in touch, again, it went to email for the negotiations, and I ended up with that journalist as a long-term client. Plus, she recommended me (via Twitter and email) to other people, who also recommended me, and I ended up with a regular client base of music journalists.

So yes, it does work. Here's how to do it.

First, make sure your profile represents you accurately

When you tweet to someone, the first thing they're going to do is look at your profile. So make sure it includes:

- Your photo
- Your full name
- Your company name
- Your URL
- What you do

How do you change your Twitter profile? On the standard Twitter website, click on the **Tools icon** (the little cog) in the top right and drop it down to get **Edit profile**.

Now you have the option to change all of your details and your **Bio**(graphy). Make sure that you get all of your keywords in, press **Save Changes** at the bottom, and you're ready to go and encourage people to look at it!

How do I search in Twitter?

At the top right of the screen, you will find a **grey box with a magnifying glass icon**. You can type any words you want to search for in here and hit **Return** to run your search.

You do need to think about your search terms and what you think people who might be searching for a cookery book proofreader (or whatever) might need. I've gone for "writing cookery book", on the grounds that if someone is writing one, they are going to need editing help at some stage. So I input that, hit **Return**, and when the results come up, I choose **All** rather than **Top** or **People you follow** - to make the results list as wide as possible.

How do I interpret the Twitter search results?

Bear in mind what you're looking for: in our example, people who are writing cookery books and might need your help. Scan down the results list, and you'll soon see some hopeful ones. I would send a quick note to people who've tweeted this kind of message:

> "My mother is writing a cookery book and I get to take the pictures of all the food hell yeah"

> "If the cookery book I'm writing had a soundtrack, this would be the title track [link]"

> "Today is a good day. I'm finally putting pen to paper and writing my first book. YES! A bloody good cookery book with a twist – naturally"

but not

> "Food writing trivia: Liberace had 7 dining rooms and wrote a cookery book"

which just mentions a cookery book, and is not really associated with someone writing one right now (note, these were real tweets, and all references to the authors can be found on the blog post).

Advanced search in Twitter

Twitter searching doesn't use wild cards, which means you can't input cook* book and get it to search for cookery book, cook book, cooking book, etc. Once upon a time, you'd have to run searches for all the different words you wanted. But now you can run Advanced Search and search for lots of different things at the same time.

Click on the cog to the top right of your search results and drop it down. You'll have an option to **Save search** (we'll look at that later) and **Advanced search**. Pick **Advanced search** and you'll be taken to the Advanced Search input screen. Here you can handily choose words that must be included in the results, and words that could be included. So, in our case, I'm saying that all tweets that Twitter finds must include the words "writing book", but they can also include any of "cooking", "cookery", "cook" and "recipe". This means that it will look for "writing book" plus any one or more of the other words.

What effect does this have on the results? Well, for example, we'll now get:

> "Gotta finish writing my cook book"

> "More than half done writing a cookbook! I love to cook and bake, and was asked by several friends to write a book! Will be done by Christmas"

Result! We'll have more results doing this than for each of lots of different individual searches, and they'll all be in one place.

(When you do this kind of search, you will see that at the top of the search screen it has written out your search as "Results for writing book cooking OR cookery OR cook..." If you're familiar with online searching, you'll recognise that this means that it's using the Boolean operators AND, OR. Of course, you can also use NOT, if you want.)

How do I save a Twitter search?

When you've found a good search that has a lot of useful results (no search will have ALL useful results, but this seems a good one), you can save the search. Click on the **cog**, drop it down and choose **Save search.**

When you next click in the search field, you will get a list of Recent searches and Saved searches. Our search is in Recent searches at the moment, but will stay in Saved searches, now you've saved it. This means that you can just click on that search query rather than typing it all in again.

How often should I re-run my Twitter job searches?

I recommend running each of your searches every 24 hours. This gives you only a few extra results each time, it's easy to note where the ones that you've already seen start and, if you want to reply to a tweet, it's not too long since the person tweeted it.

It might be worth running them more frequently at first, but keep an eye on how many new results come up during 24 hours and you'll get an idea of the schedule to use. I wouldn't leave it longer than 24 hours, for fear of missing out, as Twitter is a very immediate medium.

How do I pitch for a job on Twitter?

You might feel a bit uneasy about this. But I can promise you that no one minds one short, friendly and non-pushy contact in reply to a tweet they've sent out. I've sent loads, and I've had a certain amount of success; some people have ignored me, but no one has ever complained.

For example, as a proofreader looking for work on cookery books, I might send something like this:

"@[TwitterID] Do you need an editor for your cookbook? If so, maybe you'd like to talk. Do drop me a line if interested! Thanks!"

So, a very non-pushy, friendly and polite tweet inviting them to respond. If they did respond positively, I'd very quickly move to giving them my website URL (even though it's on my profile, I'd put it in a tweet) and initiate email contact so we could discuss the project in more detail.

Appendix 2: How to add a link to a blog post

I've talked about linking your blog post to other people, especially guest post contributors. Because many people really don't seem to know how to do this, I've added these instructions. Feel free to skip them if you already know how to do this, but it really can make the difference between a popular blog and a failed one!

Why would I add a link to a blog post?

Adding a link means that you're putting a hyperlink to either another website or another of your blog posts in the one that you're writing. There are many reasons for doing this: these are some of the reasons why I do it:

- To link a series of posts together
- To refer back to a previous post
- To thank someone for their help
- To show off something I've posted elsewhere

And, if you're reading this on an Internet-enabled device, did you notice that all of those bullet points were links to examples of what I was talking about?

A note about SEO and links (back-links)

One major advantage of links is in helping your Search Engine Optimisation (SEO). I'm not going to go deeply into that here, but basically, Google and the other search engines like to see your pages linked to on other people's pages, as it shows you're trustworthy and respected within your community enough for people to link back to you. Yes, people do try to abuse this (we've all had blog 'comments' from spammers trying to get their URL on your list of comments and now we know why) but when used properly, reciprocal linking to content that does actually interest you and is relevant for your readers does help your fellow bloggers and will hopefully lead to them linking to you, too.

How do I add a link to my blog post?

Of course, all of the blogging platforms (WordPress, LiveJournal, Blogger and others) do it slightly differently. But the difference usually comes down to the icon that they use and how much you can do once you've clicked on that icon.

I'm going to use WordPress as the main example, showing all the steps to create a link, and I'll show you what the link button looks like in Blogger and LiveJournal and, Gmail, too so you know what to look out for.

How do I add a link to a WordPress blog post?

The first thing you need to do is have some text on which you want to base the link. In the case of WordPress, there are little greyed-out icons which look like little links in a chain that are not clickable if you haven't highlighted any text. As soon as you highlight the text that you want to use as the basis of your link, the two greyed-out icons appear in all their clickable glory. One is a link, the other a link with a cross through it (for deleting links).

Keeping the text highlighted, click on the left-hand icon that looks like link in a chain. This will bring up a dialogue box for inserting your link.

WordPress allows you to do two things here; you can either link to a URL for a page outside your own blog, or you can choose one of your own previous blog posts to link to – very handy.

We're going to concentrate on linking to a URL. Type in the URL you want to link to – including http:// at the beginning.

I used to tick Open link in a new window/tab, but an experienced website manager I know got into a bit of a frenzy and told me that it's not good practice. So I do NOT recommend doing that. But whichever you choose, make sure that you're consistent.

Note: if you want to open a link in a new window or tab when you're reading a blog or web page, right-click on that link and you should get a list of options including those.

Having pressed Add Link, my text is underlined, and it will be a live link when you publish the post.

If you want to edit the link, highlight the underlined text and click on the same Link button – you can now change it as you wish.

If you want to delete the link, highlight the underlined text and click on the icon to the right, which is supposed to look like a link being broken (I think it looks more like a staple being removed).

How do I add a link to a Blogger blog post?

Blogger works in a similar way to WordPress, but the icon you need to use is the word Link, and the dialogue box doesn't give you the option to choose a previous blog post to link to, but does have the familiar URL entry field.

How do I add a link to a LiveJournal blog post?

LiveJournal uses another common icon that you'll find for a link –a globe with a link of a chain attached - and you'll get a similar dialogue box when you click that icon.

How do I add a link to a Weebly blog post?

We encounter the link / staple icon again for Weebly, this time in white on a black background.

How do I add a link to a Gmail email?

And, just because it demonstrates one of the other icons that is commonly used, if you want to add a link to a Gmail email, for example to point a friend to this blog post, the icon is another chain link / staple, but a horizontal one similar to Weebly's.

A golden rule for adding links

Wherever you add that link, make sure that it works! Test it on the live version of whatever you're publishing before you promote it.

Icons that represent adding a link

Here are those common icons again. If you want to add a link to any kind of text and you're looking for the appropriate icon on a button, it is likely to be one of these, or something similar:

To read the full version of these instructions, with all of the relevant screen shots, please pop over to my website.[50]

---

[50] http://libroediting.com/2013/06/28/add-link-to-blog-post/

Appendix 3: How to use Storify[51]

I originally wrote about Storify in response to a request from the Chinese Community Centre in Birmingham, when I was supporting them at a Social Media Surgery. You can read the full article, including all of the images and screenshots, here. In this appendix, I'm going to be talking about Storify: what is it, why would you use it, and how do you use it?

What is Storify?

Storify is a social media tool that lets you **create stories or timelines** from a variety of social media like Facebook and Twitter, as well as other web resources. It's free for the basic version, and you can use it to pull together information on whatever you want, and can customise it how you want, then share your story on the site with your friends on those social media sites.

Why use Storify?

Storify is a great way to pull together information and images and make a story that you can share with others. It's useful for events, news on particular topics, or fundraising and awareness raising campaigns. You don't have to base it around hashtags (see the chapter on Twitter above if you're not sure what these are), but doing so helps you to find related material quickly, especially now Facebook has started to use them too.

I've mainly come into contact with Storify in relation to events. For example, Karen Strunks pulls together a Storify after every Social Media Cafe in Birmingham. She gathers any Tweets and Facebook posts which have used the hashtag #bsms and creates a storyline showing the event and what people were saying about it through its

---

[51] https://storify.com/

before, during and after stages. There's an example of one of her Storify stories here.[52]

How do I join Storify?

If you're not already a member, you need to go to www.storify.com and sign up. If you don't already have an account, you need to click the **Login button** at the top right. You will be given the option to log in using Twitter or Facebook. You will still need to create a password and account with Storify: what this does is associate your Storify account with your social media account. You can choose to just create a Storify username and password.

I chose to sign up **using my Twitter account**, as that's what I use most for business and sharing. As it says, it only connects to your Twitter account and uses its authentication, it doesn't see your password etc. And when it says it will Tweet for you, that's only when you create a story, not randomly!

So, I told it my Twitter username then added my email address and a password. And that was it, I was ready to create my first story!

How do you create a Storify story?

Once you've created your account, you're ready to create a story. There's a big green button on the top row of the website, **Create Story**. Click that and you're taken to a slightly alarming page – alarming because it manages to look both blank and complicated! But little tips come up the first time you use it which guide you through what to do.

Basically you've got an area where you create your story on the left and a place to search for content on the right.

---

[52] http://storify.com/karenstrunks/birmingham-social-media-cafe-s-5th-birthday

The first thing to do is create a name for your story. You can also press the **Save Now** button at this stage, which will prompt it to autosave as you go along.

I gave my first story the edifying title "Test CBSMS story" and was now ready to add content, or **Search for elements**, as Storify calls it.

There's a row of tabs along the top – I clicked on **Twitter** and then searched for #cbsms [Central Birmingham Social Media Surgery], because I knew that that was the hashtag used around the event.

A set of Twitter results came up, all of them containing the hashtag. Storify now handily told me what to do: **drag and drop** the tweets I wanted into the story area.

This means that you can pick up particular results but not all of them – useful if some of them are repeated or just 'chatter' that you don't want to include. It also means that you can put them into whatever order you want, rather than the order imposed by the standard Twitter view (I made mine like Twitter, with the newest tweets at the top, but Karen's example has them switched it round to read from top to bottom). You **just click** on the tweet you want to include and **drag it** across into your story area.

Once I'd popped a couple of items in, I was told that I could add text. You click on the space between your items and type whatever text you want to add. So I added a note explaining some of the entries in the story which recorded me checking with one of the organisers whether it was OK to mention the event in my story.

I then hit the **Save Now** button – which I should also have done when I mentioned it earlier! Just in case!

Adding more sources to your Storify

You're not limited to creating a Storify from only one source. Along the top of the search area you can see loads of different **options**, including Facebook, Google+, YouTube, Google, and your own photos and links.

Note that if you choose Facebook, you will need to log in and link it to your own Facebook account (again, this won't do anything nasty, it just appears to need to use your own Facebook timeline. Of course, you can search for anything on Facebook once you're logged in). You don't seem to need to do that with Google+, though.

This time, I didn't bother with any Facebook items, but I did pop into **Google search** and picked up some explanatory information about the Social Media Surgery to add to my story so that is a very useful option.

How do I publish my Storify story?

The first step is to hit the **Publish button** at the top right. Just in case I had pressed it too soon, I was shown a confirmation box. I was ready to publish, so I clicked on **Publish story**.

The next step was **Share & notify**. **Sharing** creates an automated Tweet with a link to your story. I imagine that if you've signed in to Facebook, etc., you will also be given the option to post an automated status update.

Notify lets you autotweet anyone who's a friend on Twitter and is mentioned in your story to tell them that their tweet has been included in your story. I really like receiving these notifications, so I left these ticked, but you can untick them if you don't want to do this.

At this point, the story is assigned a URL that can be quoted in emails or added to your blog. In the case of this story, it was http://storify.com/LyzzyBee_Libro/test-cbsms-story, and this stays with the story on my profile for ever more.

What does my Storify look like on my Twitter account?

Storify sent an automatic tweet 'from' me with the link to my story, and then ones which told people that they'd been included. Exactly what it said it would do.

What else can I do with Storify?

When you're **searching**, you can refine your search to exclude retweets, etc.

You can get a **paid account** which is useful for large businesses or organisations. This seems to allow a lot more customisation and also real-time updates – however, I like the editable nature of the free version and I'm not sure if that would get lost if real-time updates were running. I think that most people will be OK with the free version.

About the author

I have been running my business since August 2009, moving from working freelance part time while working full time, to doing both part time, to going full time with Libro in January 2012. I've learned as I've gone along, and used social media to build my networks, and my blog and website to build her business.

You can contact me at liz@libroediting.com if you have any comments or questions about this book.

I have written several other books about careers (and cholesterol!), which are available to buy via Amazon worldwide.

My other books

All of my books are available on Amazon as well as Smashwords and other online platforms, as e-books. *How I Survived my First Full Year* is available in a print edition, too.

All about my first year of full-time self-employment, with loads of information about how I started up, how I built the business, how to know when it's time to go full-time with your part-time business, hints and tips for coping with too much — and too little — work, all the trials and tribulations, the high points and the low points.

An individual careers advice book on transcription, the area of my work most searched for and read about on my website. This book tells you all you need to know about what's involved in transcription work, the sort of work you can do,

how to tell if you're suited to it, and then shares some top tips for streamlining your work and getting the most out of it. With some general advice on freelancer life and getting freelance jobs, and handy hints for your clients when recording interviews, this gives you the all-round information you need!

This one shares how I lowered my cholesterol through diet and exercise, kept off the pills and maintained a normal cholesterol level. Packed with tips on what you can and can't eat and restaurants and brands that will help you enjoy a special meal while staying within the guidelines.

You can visit my two websites and blogs www.libroediting.com and www.lizbroomfieldbooks.com for all of the latest e-book news, as well as articles packed full of information and screen shots. I look forward to seeing you over there!

Bye for now ...

I do hope that you've enjoyed reading this book and found it useful. If you did, please go to where you bought it and post a review – it really helps independent authors like me as that's all that other buyers have to go on, and it helps my books to become visible to other people who I can help. Thank you!